**Se
Complete Wi**

WAKE UP
FROM THE INSIDE

BY JOSHUA DAVID

outskirts
press

Wake Up From The Inside
All Rights Reserved.
Copyright © 2019 Joshua David
v4.0

The opinions expressed in this manuscript are solely the opinions of the author and do not represent the opinions or thoughts of the publisher. The author has represented and warranted full ownership and/or legal right to publish all the materials in this book.

This book may not be reproduced, transmitted, or stored in whole or in part by any means, including graphic, electronic, or mechanical without the express written consent of the publisher except in the case of brief quotations embodied in critical articles and reviews.

Outskirts Press, Inc.
http://www.outskirtspress.com

ISBN: 978-1-9772-0910-8

Cover Photo © 2019 Nakia Vensel @ Creative Graphics. All rights reserved - used with permission.

Outskirts Press and the "OP" logo are trademarks belonging to Outskirts Press, Inc.

PRINTED IN THE UNITED STATES OF AMERICA

Dedication

I am dedicating this book to Our Father, Lord in Heaven, to the body of Christ, and to everyone who has the Holy Spirit inside them or will someday. I would also like to dedicate this book to my family for putting up with me during the supernatural changes in my life. Without all of you, I know I would be in the ground or in jail. I can't imagine what you all, especially my wife, have gone through. But we are going to see this through to the end, by faith and faith alone. This has made us all stronger and brought us closer to the Lord. And that's not a bad thing.

"As iron sharpens iron, so one man sharpens another" (Prov. 27:17).

I pray that our Lord Jesus Christ blesses all who read and understand these Books: to help open your spirit and soul to believe and become warriors under God.

Table of Contents

Introduction i
Unite God's Army 1
My Testimony 4
The Beginning 8
The Backslide Living Worldly 14
The Discipline from God 19
The Hand of the Lord 44
The Spirit of the Lord and His Call 60

The Prophetic Books
1 Joshua David 73
2 Joshua David 114
Amalgamations 157
1 Gentiles 172
2 Gentiles 183
3 Gentiles 193
References 199

Introduction

The purpose of this book was inspired by our Lord God, working through me, to humble and break me down in order to do His will in my life. This is a wake-up call to people in all walks of life about the importance of a personal relationship with Jesus Christ. This is for Christians of all denominations. This book also announces warning of coming judgment by Christ to our beloved country of America, and to the nations abroad.

It is my testimony, ordered by God, to tell my story and share His message. I have been a Christian since I was fourteen, and for some incredible reason I cannot explain, a switch has been turned on in my soul. Although I was about as backslidden as a Christian could be, the Lord redeemed me from the depths of pure disaster. Christ is the great redeemer. These are the things our Lord has told me to write through His Holy Spirit. He has inspired me through visions, dreams, and supernatural changes in my soul and spirit over the past few years. Our Lord is Most High, and this is a shout-out to my brothers and sisters to become serious Christians spiritually and join our fight against evil. For those who don't know Jesus, this is a call to seek Him out and realize He went to the cross and was crucified for our sins and then rose from the dead to save us from everlasting torment in the Lake of Fire. **Accept Him!** Be a child of God and join us in this fight. Time is getting short. We are entering the final push for the Church Age and gathering of God's people. We are at war! And **you** are directly in the middle of this war, whether you believe it or not. My cry to you is to accept and allow the Lord to use you in any way possible in the name of, and through Jesus Christ. Are you truly one of God's people?

Unite God's Army

It's time to unite Christian brothers and sisters and become one unit under Christ, our Savior. Fight back and destroy evil and the negative energy! The Lord said the foundation is a rock. That foundation is believing in God and believing in His son, Jesus, who died on the cross for our sins. It does not matter if you are Catholic, Lutheran, or Baptist! It does not matter if you are Presbyterian, Eastern Orthodox, or any other protestant denomination. It does not matter! We are all brothers and sisters together in Christianity. One God the Creator, one Christ our King, and one Church in the name of Jesus! We believe in the same God and believe Jesus died on the cross for our sins. Leave it at that!!

In Revelation, God states in letters, through John, to the different churches of the nations that we are *all* His people even though we may have strayed a little from the Word. Repent—God forgives. Believe—God shows grace. And most of all, rejoice—God is merciful. We all have to stand up to Satan and hang our heads high for the Most High. We must rally our troops to throw that old, filthy serpent back in his hole! The time is **now** to stop debating, stop ridiculing, and stop worrying about "that church did this" and "this denomination does that." We all believe in the same foundation. We need each other and cannot do it alone. Everyone must be on board. A crack in the armor gives way to defeat! We must keep our armor indestructible and shiny-new in the Word of God. We can defeat any number of armies and soldiers so long as we stick together and pray for our God to be with us and help us. If we unite, then we will be unstoppable!

There is nothing our God cannot do! He is the beginning and the end, the Alpha and Omega, the King of Kings! We have read stories of His greatness, saving our brothers and sisters time and time again throughout history. It will get worse before it gets better, but stay the course and allow faith to be your shield. If we stay together and keep Jesus's name in our hearts, deep within our soul, dwelling within us and throughout our ranks; Nobody can defeat us! We must stop sweating the small stuff and taking the easy way out.

Don't be ashamed that you believe in God. Don't be ashamed that we have Christ in our hearts and the light of the true God in our spirit. Fight to the death for Christ! I would gladly lay down my life to save any one of my brother or sister Saints in the name of Jesus. From the Motor City to Tokyo, from Argentina to Amsterdam, and everywhere in between, our God created all the lands. We are one! Unite the clans! The time is now, and the time is coming when the Lord will make His return. He needs us to represent! He does not care about worldly religion; all He cares about is that you opened your heart and soul to Him. He will do the rest. Trust in Him. Our Father and His mighty Angels have your back. Christ Jesus and the Holy Spirit have your back. All of us Saints got your back.

Lean on and trust your fellow Christians. We are all family. We are an endangered species! We need each other, and we *will* prevail. Praise the Lord! I love all of you, and God surely loves all of you. His love is everlasting. He will not let you down. Be steadfast in faith. Repent and believe, for we will not fail!

My Testimony

Greetings from Joshua, a persecuted Saint who has suffered for my King, Jesus Christ. For the glory of my Father, the Lord of Hosts, to honor, serve, and uphold His will in my life. I write food for my fellow Saints who belong to Christ's Church, as well as for those whom the Lord deems ripe to touch their hearts and fill them with the Holy Spirit through Jesus, Son of God. These accounts happened during the reign of Barrack Obama, President of the United States in North America. The Lord blesses all who understand and read this message in full.

Our Lord has revealed to me that we are in the final push for His people. I am writing this through God, who has literally opened my spirit and soul to see and feel things not of a natural state. "I am the way, the truth, and the life. No one comes to the Father but through Me." Jesus Christ states this in John 14 as He instructs how salvation is accomplished, and that he who believes will receive the Spirit of Truth. I am inspired by that same spirit Christ gave me; He has chosen me to lay out my nakedness for all to hear, revealing my secrets and atrocious sins along with my fleshly desires that I lusted over, which created a marriage because of my fallen nature, only to be redeemed by the love of Christ Jesus. He has plucked me out of this Earth to see, feel, and hear things not of this world, to send His message, all for the glory of God. He truly has allowed me to grow in wisdom and set my sights on the things of Heaven not of Earth. "Set your minds on things above, not on earthly things" (Col. 3:2).

I am a lifetime construction worker in concrete and landscaping. Never in my wildest dreams had I thought I would be attempting to write *anything,* let alone a book—especially something like this. I was average at best through high school and college at writing reports and essays. Trust me, my mother was the editor in chief of all my essays. However, I share compassion with many of my fellow brothers and sisters throughout history. The Lord chooses His people. Throughout the Bible it seems God has chosen many people far from having a relationship with, to do His will and work through; Paul, Jacob, and Moses to name a few. There are also men He has chosen who would be considered crazy by most, such as Samson, Ezekiel, and Solomon with his concubines.

Christ, along with the Holy Spirit, has molded me and this book to His specifications. In fact, He has changed my life so fast that when I first began to write this book, I knew only the basic Bible stories that one would learn in Sunday school. It's been thirteen years since I attempted to write anything other than checks to pay bills or a grocery list. It makes me laugh and shake my head in amazement to even be doing this, but all the while I'm praising God for giving me not only life itself, but this extraordinary story and power through His Word. And I do mean power. The Lord has amazing power. It's through

Him I am able to fight off and turn away the wicked spirits and legions of Satan's army, take back control of my own life, and write these messages by the pure grace, mercifulness, and love of God. A man of God once told me, "God must work *in* you before He can work *through* you." I love that choice of words, because it is most definitely true. I had much God needed to work inside of me.

With that being said, I pray for you. I pray that you will read and carefully listen to the words I have written because they are not my own words. They are a story and messages from the Most High, who has used a willing servant in me, to glorify Him and touch other souls—to bring children of God back from the depths of this world, as well as plant seeds in the hearts of others. . . Because play time . . . is over.

Will you take this journey with me? Will you open your mind and ask God even if you are not a believer yet? Will you ask Him to guide you through this journey, to stay focused, and to receive whatever information is needed for your life? Because this is for **you** not me! This is for you…and for our Father in Heaven.

My fellow Saints, take this ride with me. Trust in our God. Trust in Christ. Trust in my message. Climb aboard; I am your brother. I bring truth from the Holy Spirit! We need spiritual food. We need warriors. Things are not going well for our people—look outside! Look beyond your cozy homes. Expand your thoughts globally. There's a war going on. God and His army ain't playin. Satan and his army definitely ain't playin.

Look what the adversary and our own apostasy (a complete abandonment and turning away from God) are doing to our country. Get inspired; the prophecies of the last days are starting to arrive! Those of you who are born again can feel the spirit inside churning because Christ lives in you. Jesus is stirring the hearts of His people because time is short. We need you! Get on board, my fellow servants. Now is our time! Now is time for the Church to step up in the name of our King and High Priest, Jesus. We are His bride, so let's back our groom. He is coming soon!

Let me ask you a series of questions. Would you give up everything for *one chance*? Would you set aside your own fears for *one shot*? Just *one opportunity* to do what the Lord asks of you? Are you willing to put all the cards on the table? Are you willing to go *all in*? To put your personal differences aside and say, "**I don't care anymore. I must help and defend my Father and His son, Jesus. I cannot take any more of this!**" Then let Christ inspire you through my story and His messages, because it's time to **Wake-Up-Church! Wake up! Wake up from the inside!** May the Lord be with you. I love you, brothers and sisters.

The Beginning

God decided to turn on a light switch of vision inside me, a light into the spiritual world. Yes, you are reading this correctly. I said that I have been able to see and feel Holy Angels, demons, and unclean spirits, as well as wicked spirits and principalities in the heavenly places. Are you listening to me? I have seen our fellow servants who are angelic beings and messengers of the living and true God. Rejoice in that because this is real, my fellow Saints. It is going to be awesome in Heaven. Hallelujah! Therefore, without a doubt, I know Jesus Christ our God is for real, not that I didn't believe before, but I have seen and felt just a fraction of His greatness and glory with my own eyes—each time falling to my knees to worship the One who is Holy and worthy to be praised, the Lord, my God, whom I trust and live for!

That being said, I do have a downside to the beginning of my story. The Lord had allowed the hedge or wall of protection around my physical space to be cut down, so I would endure physical, mental, and spiritual suffering that I would not wish on any man. But along with it came hands-on training in spiritual warfare, discernment, and wisdom. Satan explains his case to God *in Heaven* during a meeting with accusations against Job, demanding to be allowed to test Job's faith:

"You have always put a wall of protection around him, his home, and his property. You have made him prosper in everything he does" (Job 1:10).

My protection was lifted much like Job's was and many others. Jesus tells Peter of this same type of trial in Luke.

"And the Lord said, Simon, Simon, behold, Satan hath desired to have you, that he may sift you as wheat: But I have prayed for thee, that thy faith fails not: and when thou art converted, strengthen thy brethren" (Luke 22:31-32).

You see, my friends, Satan is the great accuser and is constantly asking to test our faith before God. By God's good grace, He lifted up a standard against the evil one in my place, and that standard was refreshing compared to the standard our brother Job was given. "When the enemy comes in like a flood, the Spirit of the Lord will lift up a standard against him" (Isaiah 59:19). Are you asking yourself, "Satan visits Heaven? Isn't he in hell?" Scripture tells us no:

"Now there was a day when the sons of God (Angels in the Old Testament) came to present themselves before the Lord, and Satan came along with them. And the Lord said unto Satan, where have you come from? Then Satan answered the Lord and said, from going to and fro on Earth and from walking up and down it" (Job 1:6-7).

Of course, there's this old favorite:

"For our struggle is not against flesh and blood, but against the rulers, against the principalities, against the powers of this dark world and against spiritual wickedness in the heavenly realms" (Eph. 6:12).

Yes, there are wicked spirits in the heavenly realms. The bottomless pit is not prepared yet for many evil souls and dark spirits—until **that day** when Jesus makes His return and the Angel with the keys to the bottomless pit chain Satan up for a thousand years at the very end of the Tribulation period.

"And I saw an Angel come down from Heaven, having the key to the bottomless pit and a great chain in his hand. And he laid hold on the dragon, the old serpent, which is the devil, and Satan, and bound him a thousand years" (Rev. 20:1–2).

Satan has free roam throughout the first two Heavens, and he and his army no doubt have free roam on this planet. Remember, judgment will not take place on our world and those who belong to it until the seven-year Tribulation. The principalities, the dark rulers of the heavenly places, will also be judged when the Son of God, Jesus Christ, returns at the *end* of the Tribulation.

Back to my point: basically, I was thrown to the wolves. May I say, dear friends, that I deserved every bit of it. I made a mockery of Lord Jesus and my Father, so I was taken to the woodshed and beaten within every inch of my soul. I wasn't physically beaten or maimed—thankfully the Lord did not allow that to happen—but I suffered almost every other form of torment you can imagine. At first, I had no idea what was happening to me. I was overmatched and completely unequipped to deal with any of this newfound ability of vision. God swiftly took any fear away and gave me tolerance when encountering the sight of these disgusting, unclean soldiers of Satan. I am grateful for that gift because fear is how you fall. Fear is how you fall. Remember that in the walks of life, dear friends.

I have always been open to this phenomenon and the spiritual side of our existence. I am a follower of Christ after all. How can we be born again and baptized by the Holy Spirit without believing in the supernatural? That being said, I would like to invite you into a story of redemption, a story that proves God's love for His people, and a story of how faith in Jesus can change your life almost instantaneously. Most of all, I want to remind all of you that God will never give up on you, so don't give up on Him!

Let me start by saying, when I was young, I'd say roughly five years old, I had always been able to remember most dreams and could feel/see certain things from time to time. I remember visions or dreams of watching myself sleep at night, going into my parent's bedroom and down the stairs and throughout the house without walking— whether in the spirit or just my soul, I do not know. It seems crazy, I know, but I vividly remember these happenings to this very day. However, I adamantly remember and will never forget moving into our new house when I was eight years old around 1989.

I was fairly reluctant and nervous leaving my old friends and starting a new school. It's tough for any kid that age; your life and everything you know is turned upside down in your little world at eight years old. The first few nights in my new bedroom were pretty rough. That uneasy feeling of being timid at first was maddening. It was different inside that new house and bedroom of mine. I am an only child, so most experiences I had growing up were always on my own. As the third evening was winding down and my parents tucked me into bed, I was a little scared, but that's completely natural. As I lay in bed, I felt something different than I had ever felt before. A fear crept over me that is unexplainable. I can still feel that fear I had to this day.

All of a sudden, as I looked by the doorway, she appeared: an older woman with black hair and deathly pale skin. She stared me down without expression, and those…those eyes were just dark. I couldn't tell what she was wearing. I could see her white hands, but the outline of the rest of her was like a shadow it was so dark. I screamed with terror. I had never experienced anything like this in my life up to that point. Mom and Dad rushed in and said everything would be fine, that I was just having a nightmare, and they put me back to bed. You know the routine. But I knew right then, even as a child, that this was not a nightmare. This was different, I was wide awake. This really happened; I saw this with my own eyes. I can still see her deathly white face staring at me while I sat upright in my bed almost thirty years later. This marked my first true vision at age eight, and I would not have another until I was thirty-two.

As I mentioned earlier, I became a Christian at a young age. At fourteen I accepted Christ; I was in ninth grade. I know this for certain because I was crying facedown as I accepted Jesus as my savior during a Saturday night sermon at a youth group winter retreat. The Lord surrounded me with the Holy Spirit, convincing me of my need for Him, something I had never felt before. The following weeks confirmed it: everything seemed different. This experience is truly unexplainable, but the best way I can describe it is this: imagine all of the basic senses and emotions of your body, soul, and spirit becoming absolutely alive and connected with something higher. Therefore, a believer knows that Jesus is connected to salvation and is the true son of the Most High. Many people call this sanctification of the Spirit," an expression that defines the feeling people get when the Holy Spirit confirms you have been baptized by the Spirit, through Christ, and entered into the Holy family, making you a child of God. Others may call it the "Voice of Truth". The only possible way you can enter Heaven is to become Holy. You cannot enter the gates of Heaven without the Holy Spirit living inside you which is by accepting Christ as your Lord and savior. The very nature of our existence does not meet the standard of God; therefore, we must accept Jesus who paid the ultimate sacrifice on the cross. "Jesus told him, I am the way, the truth, and the life. No one comes to the Father but through Me" (John 14:6).

The Backslide Living Worldly

As I went through high school and college, like so many of us during those years, tolerance and acceptance of our peers were of utmost importance. I was very involved in sports and having fun—football, basketball, beer, and girls were my main attractions. As I grew older and my college career ended, I went back home to the Northeast, where I would eventually marry and have two children. Church was an afterthought at this point in my life, and I only attended a few times a year. By the time I was in my mid-twenties, my life revolved around money, beer, occasional drugs, and having a good time, in that exact order. You are the company you keep, as the saying goes, and it is quite true.

Over time, hanging with the wrong crowd and certain social circles wore me down into behaving, believing, and accepting a lifestyle that was not conductive to my salvation and walk with Christ. I drank every weekend with friends and family, watching football or other sports while gambling and playing poker, and the occasional party drugs would be involved from time to time. I never was much of a drug kind of guy for most of my life. I did like alcohol, but every once in a while, I would partake of cocaine, marijuana, and prescription drug use. My main form of idolatry worship, much like most Americans, was the love of money and possessions: Greed. As the Bible states, this is the worship of Mammon, which is the God of money and wealth.

"No man can serve two masters: for either he will hate the one and love the other, or he will be devoted to one and despise the other. You cannot serve God and Mammon" (Matt. 6:24).

Many people do not realize this is a form of idol worship, but they serve a principality without even knowing what they are doing. This is why Christ came to strip the evil rulers and principalities and redeem our souls by His blood on the cross.

"He canceled the record that contained the charges against us saints. He took it and *destroyed* it by nailing our fallen nature and sins to the cross, Christ cross. In this way, God *disarmed* the evil rulers, principalities, and authorities. He shamed them publicly by His victory, triumphing over them on the Cross of Christ" (Col. 2:14–15).

Our enemy will use any tactic possible to separate man from God the Father. This love and greed for money and possessions that outweighs love for the true living God is one of the major downfalls leading into the judgment of North America by our Lord.

In the spring of 2011, I sold out to this world. I had completely turned from God and was willing to do whatever it took to get ahead financially and chase the almighty dollar. I had abandoned Christ almost completely by this point, I believed, but did not consult Him in any facet of my life. My priorities solely depended on money, and pride. I didn't need God; I could depend on myself. I was a product of our nation; Godless, and completely turned away from the foundation this country was built upon, Christ.

I had this feeling that lasted for a day or two, the feeling of "are you really gonna do this?" I believe it was the Holy Spirit. My answer at that time was "Yes, absolutely." So I dove in head first and crossed that imaginary line into the dark world. In April 2011, I began to sell prescription drugs. Not a few here or there, no, not me; when I do something, I'm either all in or nothing at all. Like fifteen hundred to two thousand pills per week, some seven to ten thousand per month. The old saying "I knew a guy who knew a guy," that was me. I made tons of money in the beginning. I figured I had the connection, plus I knew lots of clients already. Perfect situation, right? This lasted week after week for over two years. Every Thursday or Friday was product pickup day. I'd say I wasn't small time but a mid-level drug dealer—and if I got a deal on other illegal drugs, you bet I'd sell those too—but my main business was prescription pain medicine. During this time, I was doing shady deals everywhere; as long as I made cash, it didn't matter. I owned a landscaping business, which gave me the pleasure of being my own boss, which resulted in plenty of time for illegal ways of raking in money. Stealing, embezzlement, fraud, you name it. At this time of my life, I was involved in many things I am ashamed to admit. But that's a whole other story in itself.

Like most drug dealers, after you deal for a while, you start taking what you dish out. Toward the end of the two years, I saw myself and others begin to change for the worse. Many of my clients were completely addicted to pain meds, and so was I. Many clients had already moved on to higher forms of drugs, such as heroin, which I did not deal. Over time, my supplier could not keep up with the demand, so it was getting harder to keep up the quantity I needed to fulfill orders. Plus, as I became more and more addicted, I began to get sloppy with my business and my money. The result was that I walked away from my landscaping company due to the horrible decisions effected by my distorted mind. Not to mention, I thought I was "Mr. Big Shot" and ran my company from bars, golf courses, and fancy restaurants, wasting enormous amounts of money. At some point, and I don't remember when, I started to resent dealing drugs and the whole wannabe gangster life. So after feeling this way for a while, I decided to stop and take a few days to do some soul-searching and reflect on what I had become.

By April 2013:

1. I had lost my entire lawn care company.
2. I had dealt poison to my clients contributing to their dependency on drugs.
3. I was addicted to painkillers and Suboxone (a substitute for opiate-based drugs that help ease withdrawal), taking up to twenty Vicodin per day.

4. The money I was making dried up, leaving me with less money coming in than going out, because of my own dependency and poor decisions.

Slowly, over the course of a month, I had a change of heart about dealing drugs. I saw what it was doing to people, and I started to feel responsible in a big way for contributing to many clients' downfall, as well as my own. I was being convicted from above, now that I look back on it. I did not realize it then, but I know the Lord was talking to me through His Spirit. So I cut my orders in half each week over the course of a month. Then, after about six weeks, I completely quit selling drugs and only fed my own addiction.

Not a day goes by I don't feel horrible that I dealt this poison. I was part of the problem. I was working for the enemy. I feel so sorry and would like to apologize to everyone, especially those who are still on that train or have gotten worse. From the bottom of my heart, I'm deeply sorry and feel responsible for those who are still lost. I contributed to the downfall of many people I care about. I feel ashamed to this day. I was a loser.

The Discipline from God

So there I was at thirty-two: married with two children, addicted to pain meds, smoking two packs of cigarettes a day, and unemployed. I had just quit the very job that I had sold my entire landscape company for one year previously, when my life as I knew it began to change forever. Honestly, I still thought I was in control. Well, I found out the hard way that I was *not* in control. God was.

What happened to me in the summer of 2013 was supernatural and completely different than anything I could ever imagine or comprehend at the time. I believe the Holy Spirit, or an Angel of the Lord touched me inside. Turning my switch or light into the spiritual world completely on, which I'd had few glimpses of as a child. I always kept an open mind because any and all things are possible through God. However, this was an ability inside me that lay dormant until the opportune time, when God directly intervened and used my life in order to fulfill a particular job.

July 2013

I was lying in bed with my wife on a Friday night, watching a little TV before going to sleep. I remember we were watching *Dateline on NBC*. I was starting to get tired, so I rolled over onto my back to get comfortable. I turned my head slightly to the left and there she was: a Caucasian woman with dark brown hair standing at my bedpost. She was watching TV. She turned her head, looked right at me, and nonchalantly turned her head back to continue watching *Dateline*. In amazement I slowly turned to my wife and whispered, "Did you see that?" She asked, "See what?" I said, "The woman by the bedpost watching TV with us!" My wife looked at me as if I was crazy. The woman had disappeared by this point. I was absolutely sure of what I saw and was adamant about the situation, so we decided to get up and see if my mother-in-law was awake. She had been living with us for a little over three years. We searched the main floor of the house, but nobody was there. We went to the basement where her bedroom was, and my mother-in-law was fast asleep in bed. I knew I wasn't crazy; I had seen this woman. My old lady still thought I was nuts. But that's beside the point; she always thinks I'm nuts.

The woman I had seen seemed to be peaceful, and I felt no feelings of fear or negativity at the time. She simply was watching TV as if she did this every night with us. Even when she turned to me, it was as if she was just looking over to see what my wife and I were doing and if we had fallen asleep.

Eventually we went back to bed, and a few minutes went by. As I lay in bed trying to figure out what had happened, thinking maybe I had fallen asleep and was dreaming, I looked to the left and saw a younger man, probably in his early to mid-twenties, leaning over my wife across the bed. With a look of amazement on his face, he was waving his hands wildly as if to get my attention. This time I jumped out of bed and said, "Did you see *that*?" My wife said in an aggravated voice, "Now what?" I replied, "There was a young guy standing on your side of the bed, leaning over you and waving his hands at me trying to get my attention!" Now she started to believe something was going on and began to get a little scared. Both visions lasted approximately two seconds each and then vanished. It took me a while to fall asleep that night, as you can imagine, but that would be the only visions I had for the rest of the evening.

A few days went by and I began to disregard what had happened. Out of sight, out of mind. Little did I know that this was just the beginning of my journey into the spiritual realm.

People who have these abilities attract more attention from spirits and souls than the average individual without these abilities. The spirits/souls can establish better communication with a living person who is more open to this realm. When I saw the first lady by the bedpost, it triggered a chain reaction. Once you notice them, the spirits or souls are aware that you notice them and are drawn to that individual; like an insect being drawn to the light (pun very intended).

I am going to clear up something right now before I go on. For a child of God, to be out of the body is to be present with the Lord. "We are confident, I say, and willing rather to be absent from the body, is to be present with the Lord" (2 Cor. 5:8). I don't want people to think I am suggesting that those who have received the Holy Spirit and are dead in Christ are not with Christ in Heaven. They absolutely are with the Father in Heaven. I am speaking of the souls of the departed, and those who did not receive the Holy Spirit, ones who rejected Jesus Christ while living in their earthly body.

Throughout the Bible, God gives multiple examples of people who have this vision. Not all are used for good; that's where false prophets, sorcerers, and witchcraft come into play.

"He made his son pass through the fire, practiced witchcraft and used divination, and dealt with mediums and spiritists. He did much evil in the sight of the Lord provoking Him to anger" (2 Kings 21:6).

This was during the reign of King Manasseh, who ruled the southern Kingdom of Israel (Judah), during the time when the great Assyrian Empire controlled northern Israel, sometime between 700 and 650 BC. He set up temples for Baal (the sun god), and Ashtoreth/Astarte (the great mother or nature goddess generally associated with the moon). What's even more grotesque and despicable is that this form of worship included a god named Moloch. Citizens who belonged to this religion would sacrifice their own infants and small children to Moloch by burning them in ovens or over hot coals.

This is a great depiction of how people with sight, or *seers* as the Bible states, can falsely turn people toward terrible religions or confusion detestable to the Lord. These false prophets speak from familiar spirits and demons. They do not pray to the one true God of Israel and Jesus Christ for their information. Many of today's psychics are perfect examples of false seers and false prophets. They only tell people what they want to hear and speak to the dead.

"They say to the seers, see no more visions! And to the prophets, give us no more visions of what is right! Tell us pleasant things, prophesy illusions and lies" (Isa. 30:10).

They use their ability for Satan without knowing, and most of all, for profit/gain. Many do not even realize it, but they are confused by lies. They have either been deceptively tricked into believing certain lies or have accepted particular familiar spirits into their personal space. Most are working under the mother of harlots, the great prostitute, who sits over false religion of this world (Rev. 17).

These pagan mediums, psychics, and other people who use extrasensory perception (ESP), and practice readings and other forms of spiritual rituals receive their information from spirits who have not confessed that Jesus Christ has come in the flesh. They are the minions of certain evil rulers in the Heavens under Satan's kingdom. The apostle John states in 1 John:

"By this you know the Spirit of God: every spirit that confesses that Jesus Christ has come in the flesh is from God. Every spirit that does not confess Jesus has come in the flesh is not of God: and this spirit is of the antichrist. You have heard that he is going to come into the world, and he is already here" (4:2–3).

The true seer, prophet, or person with the ability must discern from evil/deception messages, and messages coming from the true Creator, Father God. This is one of the spiritual gifts from the Holy Spirit that the apostle Paul states in I Corinthians:

"He gives one-person power to perform miracles, to another prophecy, to another *distinguishing between spirits*, to another speaking in different kinds of tongues, and to another interpretation of tongues" (12:10).

Over the course of several months, I had tormenting nightmares. It was getting more and more disturbing. I actually had begun to talk in my sleep, according to my wife. We had been married for over twelve years, and I had never been a sleep talker before. I had no idea at the time that this had started, but as time went on, it got worse. I realized how serious it had become when I woke up in the middle of night and in a deep voice that didn't seem like my own, I (or it) said loud and stern, "You will do what I say!" It startled my wife so badly that she couldn't sleep the rest of the night. I was stunned at first because I had been in a complete sleep, and to wake up yelling this was like something out of a horror film. A few minutes went by and I began to laugh it off. I went back to bed while my wife continued to turn and look at me as if I were possessed. In hindsight, this was the beginning of true demonic forces taking a hold on me without my realizing it.

September 2013

Things were starting to become very dark. Depression had set in, my mind was foggy, and I could not seem to get my bearings on life. Another advancement or step in my ability had started to evolve. When I closed my eyes at night and started to get comfortable in bed, I would have flashes of people and faces I had never seen before or had known in my lifetime. Can you imagine lying on your couch, closing your eyes, and after thirty seconds, seeing instant projections of faces and people doing certain motions and distorting to evil forms? Not one vision, but wave after wave of these visions. In a twenty-second time frame, eight or nine projections would appear as a picture in my mind. I would see a split-second snapshot, never lasting more than two seconds. They were evil. Some of the faces would look normal before distorting into terrible, frightening faces with their mouths turning into devilish smiles or things much worse. Maybe one out of ten of these visions would be a natural-looking person.

Over time I would find out that the ones who appeared normal and friendly were actually familiar spirits that our Holy Bible teaches us about time and time again. This happened on a nightly basis—wave after wave of these visions. I would try to daydream about what took place during the day or conversations I had earlier that day—anything to take my mind somewhere else and possibly stop this nightmare when trying to fall asleep. Nothing worked. They would come one after another after another until I opened my eyes for a few seconds and tried to shake them off. Then I would close my eyes again for a minute or two, begin to get relaxed, and they would start all over again. I battled this every single night. I would pray for God to let me have peace during the really bad nights. Sometimes it worked and other times it didn't. At this point in my life, I had not completely turned back to the Lord and repented. Even when praying worked, a few hours would go by and I would wake up, roll over in bed, and the whole process would start all over again, or I would have awful night terrors. Not a bad dream, I mean night terrors. The dreams you never forget from the fear that goes deep inside.

I thought I was going crazy. I would begin to get angry, furiously angry, and literally want to tear the spirits apart. Some nights I wouldn't be able to fall asleep for hours. I could talk to my wife about what was happening to me, but I felt totally embarrassed to tell anyone else at this time. Once again, my relation to Job is a great parallel. He too went through this tactical warfare with Satan because of his absolute alliance and faith in God. "You scare me with dreams, and terrify me with visions" (Job 7:14). As I said earlier, God had lifted certain walls of protection around me, much like he had done to Job, allowing the enemy to infiltrate.

This was beginning to take a huge toll on me—night after night seeing these phenomena, constantly waking up in the middle of the night, and not being able to go back to sleep. I didn't know what to do; I thought I was going insane. Maybe I needed to see a psychiatrist or go to a psych ward, I thought many times. Somehow, and only God knows why, when I began to relax, my soul or mind opened up in the spiritual realm, allowing me to catch glimpses of what was taking place in and around my surroundings. Some call this meditation, ESP, or channeling; at this time of my life, I called it a curse. Drinking alcohol at night only made things worse. I was able to fall asleep, but I would be woken up by nightmares and tormented in the middle of the night. The demonic oppression kept getting worse. I was confused and honestly tortured every day. I had no idea what to do, and I certainly, at that time, couldn't talk to anybody about my problems. People would think I was insane. How embarrassing, I thought. The last thing I wanted was to come off to friends and family as psychotic or mentally unstable.

This type of reaction is common for many people who are demonically oppressed and possessed. There is a major difference between the two. Possession is extremely rare. Demonic possession occurs when a malevolent spirit or demon, takes possession of an **unholy** spirit, resulting in control over the original host of the body. Demonic oppression is much more common and has to do with demonic influences in your life through the flesh, fallen nature, generational curses, and accusations by the enemy, Satan. The few times I tried to reach out to close friends and family outside of my box resulted in complete disaster. Either my relationship with the person would become distant, or the individual would act as if I had never said a single word about what was taking place in my life spiritually, which made me feel even more uncomfortable and ostracized.

As If I didn't have enough problems with spiritual issues, addiction to pain meds, and smoking two packs of cigarettes a day, I started to throw cocaine use into the mix as well. I was extremely depressed and confused. I was looking for any type of escape. This decision would take me into months of darkness from which only prayer and faith in Christ would lead me out.

October 2013

A light went off in my head after the first few times I used coke. I didn't have many visions and would rarely have spiritual issues when I went to bed. I found the more cocaine I did, my ability to see into the paranormal world became less and less. Plus, I enjoyed it. At first cocaine was awesome. I was able to have tons of energy to do daily tasks, and it took me away from being depressed, or so I thought. I was able to fall asleep normally, although it would take a while (cocaine is an extreme upper), without any visual problems. I started using one or two days a week. When I went without coke, every night was the same thing over and over again. These monsters of evil would appear to me. I was becoming more and more depressed and desperate about my situation. So I started using more and more often; it gave me a coping mechanism and an escape from reality. As I said, I started using two days a week, which slowly turned into three and then four days a week. Before I knew it, a little over a month had gone by and I was completely addicted to cocaine. Isn't that just great!

I don't know what it was, but when I used, I was unable to enter that state of mind or relax as I would normally do while sober and see into the spiritual realm. Apparently, I am the complete opposite from the norm; most people see things or hallucinate while doing drugs. Go figure. After a little over a month, I was a full-blown cokehead and addicted to pornography. For me, using cocaine and watching porn went together like peas and carrots. Using drugs and visiting porn websites was an everyday part of my life. This went on for almost eleven months. I didn't know how to deal with this severe demonic oppression in any other way. I kept spiraling out of control. I had enough issues to deal with, and now I had added two more addictions to the list. By Thanksgiving 2013, I was spending an average of $500 a week on cocaine.

This was the life I was dealing with every day, and the only way I knew how to deal with it, was escaping through drugs. Unknown to me at the time, I had allowed the demonic forces and addiction spirits to enter and influence my judgment and my will. The demons were winning. My life was in complete shambles. Between November 2013 and March 2014, my life had reached rock bottom. It was the darkest six months imaginable, with no feeling of hope.

My wife figured out what I had been doing for the past several months. I was a joke of a father to my son and daughter. I had neglected them as well as my whole family. I became a hermit, completely unsocial, a shell of my former self. My total selfishness and lack of compassion for anyone but myself had reached an all-time high. I literally didn't care about life anymore. I was ready to give up; I was done. My wife and I were on the verge of divorce and the total uprooting of our lives. This was the worst period of my entire life. I still feel disgusted with myself and so ashamed. It makes me sick to my stomach when I think how confused and misguided my thoughts were.

March 2014

My life was on the verge of total collapse. I thought to myself, this can't be my life. I was an emotional wreck. I knew I couldn't sit back and continue down this path, but I could not conquer the demonic activity and my addictions on my own. The enemy was feeding off of me, and the demonic oppression was so intense that I stood no chance in this battle. I had had enough. I reached the point at which I had absolutely nowhere else to turn except to Christ, or I was going to give up on life. I was defeated in every way.

So I went back to the basics, which for a Christian are the basic fundamentals of our faith. I started praying—a lot—and I even started reading the Bible for the first time in my life.

This was the beginning stages of turning back to God in my life, mentally and spiritually—something I know the Lord was waiting for me to do. Like a boxer and his trainer, God had stripped me of all I knew, every bit of my will and control, so I would stop doing things my own way and start letting Him train and fight some battles within me. Finally, I started to hear His voice again.

A few weeks went by, and I felt for the first time a pure desire to stop using drugs. When it comes to addictions, there must be a desire to quit before things will begin to move forward. It's not just saying out loud that you want to stop; it must be a burning desire deep inside that says, "I must quit." There is a big difference between "want to" and "must do"! I was so far into my addictions, coupled with this new ability to see into the spiritual realm, that I simply could not do this on my own. I was way overmatched to take on all of this without Christ. Frankly, it was all still too much for me to comprehend at this time of my life, but slowly, over the course of the next few months, I cut my cocaine use in half. Using two to three days a week, as opposed to five to six days a week, for me was a step in the right direction.

This, however, came with a price. Satan took notice. As I started turning to the Lord and slowly scaling back my addictions, my visions started getting stronger. I was seeing more and more demonic activity in and around me. It got to the point that no matter if I drank alcohol or used drugs, I would have visions and wild, tormenting dreams. Satan was upping his game because he knew I was seeking truth and was on the right path, the path that led to victory through Jesus Christ.

My increasing visions of entities and other supernatural phenomena advanced more and more into this world of confusion. I was addicted to cocaine, Suboxone, and cigarettes, and I was unbelievably depressed. Although I had cut my cocaine use in half, I was still going up the creek without a paddle. I had allowed too many doors to be opened in my life for Satan to enter. I was letting him get the best of me. Still I pressed on with prayer and reading my Bible; it truly was the only thing I could do. I had nowhere else to turn.

Sometime towards the end of April 2014, I began to feel for the first time God's power through His Word. I was praying every day. Some days I would win my battle with our enemy and some days I lost, but I had started to win for the first time in years. The main victory was having the foundation of Christ back in my life. When small victories are made through God, expect Satan to recognize this and come back with a powerful blow to discourage you. And that's exactly what happened.

I was going through a small transition period. My drug use was dwindling, along with my porn addiction. At this point in my life, I was winning more days a week than I was losing against both addictions. As this was happening, a deep hatred and anger started brewing inside me. I was furious at these demonic beings and developed a hatred for any evil people. I was so sick and tired of seeing, feeling, and dealing with these entities. I was ready for revenge. Imagine trying to take a nap during the day, then hearing two spirits taunt you with vulgar language and blasphemies, then projecting the most gruesome putrid images imaginable for fifteen minutes behind your closed eyes before you would fall asleep, *every single day* for a year. I had had it! My fuse was short, and I was ready to explode. I wanted some payback time, and I wanted to inflict pain on anything or anyone associated with evil. I had the door *wide open* for another enemy to infiltrate my space. In fact, I flagged it right in. Hate was its name. I was confused, desperate, and totally unprepared for what was about to take place.

May 2014

Hate that I didn't know existed began to store up inside me. I mean, the thought of anything evil made me want to throw down. I played football and other physical sports while growing up and was always the physical type. I'm usually not one to back down from escalated situations, but I was starting to lose it. I was putting my game face on for these things every night. I got to the point where I was taunting the demonic spirits and souls and threatening them right back. By this time my ability had evolved to where I could hear these spirits talk. I looked at this as a war. Not a good idea. Trust me.

Of course, I continued to pray constantly. I thought to myself, there must be a reason why this is happening to me, or there must be something I have to do. I was still in a knockdown, drag-out fight against my addictions, and now I was furious at everyone and everything. I was lost and wanted, no, *needed* closure desperately.

One morning a single thought crossed my mind, a terrible, awful thought: I would kill these demons. I would exact revenge somehow, some way. Not revenge on supernatural demonic spirits but on real, live, demon-like people. Human traffickers, pimps, drug dealers, and thieves; corruption in law enforcement and politicians—these were my targets. What a wonderful idea, I thought. I pondered this for over a week, and after that, I was all in. Going to jail or winding up dead did not matter to me at this point. My life as I saw it was ruined. I was a drug addict. I was having crazy spiritual issues, and I was starting to go completely insane. I knew that I was going crazy, but I didn't care. I was done and ready for war. Every man has his breaking point. I was getting close to mine.

This form of demonic oppression is exactly how many of today's binge murders take place—the type of murders where some random person just opens fire inside a school or at a beach, or goes on a killing spree out of nowhere. Many, I believe, are either demonically possessed or under extreme demonic oppression. In my case, I had been under severe demonic oppression, completely depressed, addicted to drugs, and entirely lost socially. Add hate and wrath into the mix, and well, it was a recipe for disaster. Satan used this hate against me to confuse and dig my hole even deeper. I was just starting to dig my way out when the wiles of the devil sucked me right back in, burying me further.

As I said before, I was totally at my wits end, so bear with me here because it gets a little nuts. I was still praying, reading the Bible, and hoping that somehow a resolution was near. I took it upon myself to create my own solution if God didn't step in. At the end of May and into June 2014, I started studying crime spots in the major city where I lived on the Internet, as well as scouting certain areas on the east side of the city. My hometown is notorious as one of the largest and most crime-ridden cities in American history. Human trafficking makes me sick to my stomach, and this particular city ranks very high in this category as well as in the top ten for just about every major crime category you can think of, year in year out.

After a couple weeks of scouting, I had discovered multiple drug houses. I had narrowed my search to two spots that I would hit up first. I figured these would be easier targets for my first few jobs. I scouted them for a couple of weeks, tracking their systems and seeing what time of day would be easiest to bust in. These were busy places. Most customers knocked on the door, and a man would be sitting by the door at all times like a fast-food drive-thru for your drug of choice. What made me choose these specific houses was the fact that I knew of people who went to these homes, and I knew exactly how their operations worked. Meanwhile, I stocked up on bullets, cleaned my guns, and put a scope on my rifle and laser sights on my hand guns. I made sure I had plenty of buck shots and slugs for my twelve-gage shotgun. I purchased certain tactical clothing and boots, so I would be prepared for any and all circumstances. I bought a couple knives for emergency purposes. I had two sets of pepper spray in undetectable container key chains. As this was all taking place, mind you, I was still battling my addictions, doing drugs a few times a week.

I read old local newspapers to find out where certain types of crimes took place and where the problem spots were. Like many major cities, in certain neighborhoods all you have to do is drive down any street and see what type of action is taking place. I knew where I would start. I was sick of everything, especially corrupt cops. I read countless articles and watched numerous TV channels, learning that drugs and money in evidence rooms were constantly coming up missing at the police stations. I watched the police raid drug houses only to recover $250 and report unusually small amounts of dope. It was a joke. They would have gotten more cash and product from me during my days of dealing than from some of the major houses they raided, and I was barely a mid-level drug dealer.

I was prepared. There were only a couple of guys at each of these drug homes. My plan was to wait until two of them left the house, which seemed to happen during the morning hours. Mornings were the slow periods of the operation. I could walk right up, knock on the door, wait for it to open, and shoot the guy point-blank in the head before he could even open his mouth. I'd take all the cash and burn all the drugs, so nobody could use or sell them again. This would be my first two jobs, and I had other ones on my radar. Not a very elaborate plan, I know, but I didn't care. If it didn't work, oh well. If I died or went to jail, that was totally fine with me too. That's the state of mind I was in then. I was completely out to avenge for myself and the Lord.

I slowly stockpiled ammo and got ready for my war on evil. I prayed and read my Bible patiently, or so I thought. I waited to receive signs of confirmation or messages from God. Having no answer, I started getting angry with Him for not answering right away and giving me guidance concerning when and where to go. So I prayed more and tried to wait and see what/when God wanted me to start. I truly believed I would be justified in my actions. My perception was so diluted that I honestly felt the reason this spiritual awakening happened to me was to do this exact thing. That's how distorted and confused I was at the time—truly under severe demonic oppression.

My hate grew more intense every night because I would see and hear these spirits. My rage and anger grew uncontrollable. I did not care. I was prepared to spend the rest of my life in jail or die doing it. Whatever I had to do in order to kill these types of people, avenging was my only thought. I was mad at the world. I created my own prison, so to speak, but that didn't matter to me at the time. I figured if I went to jail, I could just murder more people there, and it would be even easier. A prison has a bunch of evil all in one spot. What better place to kill them? Better yet, hopefully someone would murder me and put me out of my misery. How I wished to die so many times. I was not having suicidal thoughts, praise the Lord, because I knew as a Christian that would not be a good choice. But I was definitely looking to go out in a blaze of glory.

When you are physically, mentally, and spiritually exhausted, I guarantee you will beg and wish to die. Elijah wished to die: "I have had enough, Lord," he said. "Take my life; I am no better than my ancestors" (1 Kings 19:4). After Elijah killed the prophets of Baal, Jezebel, the queen of Israel, threatened his life. Elijah was defeated mentally, physically, and spiritually. Job repeatedly wished to die and so did Moses after leaving Egypt. The prophet Jonah did after he spent three days in the whale. His job was to turn the people of Nineveh, the capital of the mighty Assyrian empire, back to the Lord because He was about to judge the nation. The Assyrians were one of the most brutal and opposing empires in history. They would sack a town, completely destroy it, and round up all the men they had captured. Then they would murder them, rape the women and take them as slaves and wives, and just leave all the children behind.

Poor Jonah hated the Assyrians; he wanted no part in saving these types of people. They were evil, and he *wanted* them to be judged. Jonah wished to die after he preached God's word to the Ninevites, and they actually turned to the Lord. "Therefore now, O Lord, please take my life from me, for it is better for me to die than live" (Jonah 4:3). He turned that city to the Lord, and the people would prosper for another 150 years until the Prophet Nahum would prophecy against them on the Lord's behalf. I suggest everyone read the little forgotten book of Nahum because our beloved country is eerily similar to Assyria. And don't tell me the Old Testament doesn't matter and that it's outdated. If it is written in the Bible, it is just as important as any other book in scripture. We can learn a lot from the old judgments of nations past in our Bibles. Our great country is headed in the same direction as some of those ancient empires. Judgment will be coming soon to our nation, and we are at the beginning stages now.

July 2014

During the past few months, things were escalating, and I would see different types of demonic entities and hear them speaking from time to time. I was seeing or hearing them during naps, at night, or anytime I closed my eyes for more than a minute. As I said before, when I started to turn back to God, the adversary (Satan) retaliated. I became unable to do day-to-day tasks. I hadn't been able to act normal since the beginning of this whole thing, but it was getting worse and was affecting my family. Our house was broken, and everyone was confused and on edge. Something was terribly wrong with me, and we had to, *had to* figure this out!

Through everything, my wife had my back. What a blessing she is. She still loves me just as much as the day we got married, and she wanted to help me. She did not give up on me. She could have left when I was addicted to coke, she could have left because she thought I was insane, and she could have left when it wasn't a good environment for my children, but she didn't. I had not told her my recent plans for scouting and planning a rampage, but she knew of everything else going on in my life. She was there every step of the way. She stayed the course.

My mind was made up that I was going to murder these despicable people. It had been almost three months, and I was done waiting for God to give me a sign or answer. In my confused mind, I was ready physically and mentally. I didn't care anymore. Everything was intensifying; things were coming to a boil. A few times my wife suggested that maybe I should go talk to a psychic or medium at one of the pagan spiritual stores not too far from our house. We knew of a few places that offered readings and sold certain products for healers and other forms of pagan spiritual items. We both knew that a psychiatrist, counselor, or even the common church would not be able to help me. I had tried the church route a couple of times. Each time it left me feeling even more lost and secluded than before I went there. Being shunned or ignored and not taken seriously by those few churches was heartbreaking and debilitating.

It's a shame that we, as the Church, have allowed this to happen. We have allowed most of the people with special abilities like mine and people who are genuinely under demonic oppression or possession to slip through the cracks into Satan's hands. It seems he has all the prophets and people with these types of ability working for his army. We as the Church must reclaim, accept, and help the ones who come asking for assistance in these matters. At least the Catholic's have a system in place for this demonic oppression and possession. But when you are not a confirmed Catholic, where do you go? We shouldn't turn them away because we don't understand or know how to help them. A church gave me a 1-800 hotline number on one occasion. A hotline number? Really? I don't believe the standard counselor would have a clue what to do or say in matters like these. What if I was possessed by a demon? What is the hotline person going to do? Do you know how hard it is to come out of your comfort zone and talk with someone about a problem like what I went through? It is the most uncomfortable and embarrassing conversation ever, and when you get turned away as if you are crazy, you are left feeling completely helpless and hopeless. That's why so many turn to the pagans! At least they sit down, understand, and listen to you. That's how we lose them! We need our own prophets and children of God with these abilities! Jesus our King spent half His ministry casting out demons and healing the sick. This is real!

"And when He called His disciples to Him, He gave them power over unclean spirits, to cast them out, and to heal all kinds of sickness and all kinds of disease" (Matt. 10-1).

We need soldiers in God's army who have these abilities and gifts! We have to stop turning them away as if they are crazy or trying to disrupt the Church! Just because they have this ability does not make them witches! Do I sound like a witch? I'm a son of God! I am a follower of Christ! I proclaim Christ is who and what I stand for! A witch doesn't confess that Christ is Lord and has come in the flesh. I get so upset when I think about other people who have gone through similar circumstances and are lost. It makes me weep because I know what they are going through. It is hell, especially for Christians because they are getting persecuted spiritually. Persecution can happen in many ways to Saints with abilities like these. We are tormented every week in the realm of the spirits. Every single week I must cast out some spirit, demon, or soul from my home. Multiple times per week! As I mentioned before, they are like flies!

So I beg all of you, brothers and sisters, put your hand out to people like this. Be compassionate and help them. The Lord said He would pour out His Spirit. This is going to happen to more and more Saints before Christ takes His Church to be caught up (raptured) with Him. We are entering the last generation and coming of age. The enemies' days are numbered.

"I will pour out My Spirit upon all people. Your sons and daughters will prophesy. Your old men will dream dreams. Your young men will see visions. In those days I will pour out My Spirit even on servants, men and women alike" (Joel 2:28–29).

Back to the story. . .

I knew as a Christian that consulting spiritists and mediums was forbidden in God's Word. The Lord says multiple times in different chapters and books of the Bible specifically not to visit sorcerers, witches, or mediums:

"Do not defile yourselves by turning to mediums or those who consult the spirits of the dead. I am the Lord your God" (Lev. 19:31).

"Someone may say to you, 'Let's ask the mediums and those who consult the spirits of the dead. With their whisperings and mutterings, they will tell us what to do.' But shouldn't people ask God for guidance? Should the living seek guidance from the dead?" (Isa. 8:19).

I had also been taught by my family time and time again not to be involved in those practices. They warned me that sometimes you could bring back certain phenomena or spirits that are unwanted. I can hear my mother's and grandmother's voices right now, reaming me about going to false seers who only tell half-truths. I had never in my life talked to a psychic or medium, nor had I ever stepped foot in a pagan store. I was reluctant to do so because I knew that I would be doing evil in the sight of the Lord. By the same token, I didn't know where else to turn. The Church turned me away multiple times. I needed help and I needed help fast.

The Hand of the Lord

July 31 - August 10, 2014

It was Thursday, July 31, my scouting and preparation for the drug house attack was all set. I just needed a few more days until I would strike. I was leaving for vacation with my kids to visit my parents on Tuesday, August 5, the following week. My plan was to hit the first house on Monday and then head out on the road early Tuesday morning.

Later on Thursday, around noon, my wife called me and asked if I wanted to meet her for lunch. She had mentioned at breakfast that she was only working a half day. I agreed, so we met at Chili's. About midway through our lunch, she brought up the topic again that maybe I should visit the pagan spiritual store, just to talk to someone who could relate to what I was going through and maybe he or she could help. She said she would come with me for support. I thought, well, maybe I should. I'm not getting a reading, just talking to them. They possibly could give me some sort of explanation or information, or at least steer me in some direction. What could it hurt? So after lunch we headed over to the place, which we had passed a thousand times before.

When we arrived, I felt awkward and nervous about bringing up anything remotely close to something like this, especially to people I did not know. To this day I have not told many people about my situation—having visions and experiences into the spiritual world. It is an awkward conversation. As I mentioned before, when I open up to most people, it is an uncomfortable experience for both parties, making things awkward and leaving me frustrated and feeling stupid. Most people do not know what to say, and when the words start to come out of my mouth, it sounds wild and insane to them. People are afraid of what they don't understand.

However, at the store I finally mustered up enough marbles to ask some questions. Both of the women who worked there immediately started talking and explaining certain things as if they had counseled people like me a million times. They explained that many people were having similar spiritual awakenings; just in the last year three to five people per week had walked in the door asking the same type of questions I was asking. The number one reason, believe it or not, according to these women, was that since the planetary alignment on December 21, 2012, a multitude of people had become more sensitive and open to the spiritual world. Many seers or people with sight are called sensitives. But the great Mayan calendar planetary alignment was a hoax. The planets were never aligned on this day; it was all a big lie. Not only were these women deceived but many other people including myself also had accepted the Mayan calendar alignment, until I did my research on it.

The real reason people are having these awakenings, visions, and dreams is because our Lord Jesus will be making His return soon. He is trying to light a fire in many hearts and warn people. Our adversary is using this opportunity to work overtime, using his deception and lies. Don't believe him! That Wicca practice has Satan's name written all over it, my children! You are messing with things you do not understand and have been deceived. Come to Christ! He alone can guide you in your spiritual journey with truth! The Holy Spirit gives truth! He is your guide!

The two women talked to my wife and I for almost an hour. They explained things in a new and different way I was not used to. Also, they were adamant about being neutral, not claiming to be good or bad. In fact, when we talked about certain spirits, they refused to call anything evil. They explained that I needed to be careful about proclaiming my faith as a Christian because it could have a bad effect on my abilities, which could lead to attacks. I had made my stance on Christ clear at the beginning of our conversation. They sure got the attack part right. I'll give them that.

Many who practice pagan spiritual healing or readings are under the control of certain spirits. They fear that proclaiming Jesus Christ has come in the flesh will cause them to be attacked spiritually. They have been confused and are bound by fear, as well as lying spirits and familiar spirits. Accepting certain pagan beliefs opens the door for different realms of spirits to move in, depending on who or what principality they have accepted. The truth is Christ. Proclaiming Him in everything I do has begun an all-out assault against me by the enemy. This happens to all who believe in Christ. It is written that we will be persecuted for our testimony of Christ. This can be persecution mentally, physically, or spiritually; through the flesh, world, or demonic warfare. Satan uses all three tactics. The Lord has chosen me to be a seer for Him, not the enemy, so I simply try my best to do what the Father asks of me. I make mistakes as I go, but I have the foundation in Christ to cling to in times of trouble. And He gives me comfort in His love by following truth and knowing that I am working for His glory. Therefore, when I am attacked because of my love of Christ and truth, I know by my persecution that as one with the Lord, we are landing spiritual blows to our enemy, Satan, in the fight for the souls of man.

These two false seers at the store were surprisingly nice and took time out of their busy day to speak with me. That hour was a lot to handle, and I needed time to process all the information they gave me. I thanked them, and they gave my wife and I a hug as we said our good-byes. Like I said, both women were very kind and truly were, in their minds, just trying to help me. This is why we need to be careful of the deceptive tactics of Satan. As we were driving home, my wife and I discussed many things and continued talking throughout the night.

That evening we watched a movie, and around 10:30 p.m. we went to bed. As I lay in bed watching the nightly news, I felt something different. There was a heavy feeling of dread in the room. My wife had already fallen asleep, and I had begun to close my eyes. Then *bam*! It hit me. As I closed my eyes, instantly I was inside a car driving at top speed. I looked up and twenty feet in front of me was a guard rail with caution cones and a solid cinder block wall behind it. I was a mere twenty feet from the rail and wall, with absolutely no time to react, when the vision started. I opened my eyes right before I was about to slam into the rail and wall. I was terrified. My heart was racing, and I said a few choice words that our Lord Jesus would have given me a whuppen for.

It was like a "game-on" sucker punch before the battle started. It was the most direct vision I ever had up to this point in my life. I tried to compose myself and relax. Then I closed my eyes once again. Immediately, the most lucid vision of a demonic spirit I had ever seen came upon me. This hellish being was insane. Its head was shaking violently, and its body was twitching. The most evil smile imaginable was on its face. When a demon's mouth looks fake and moves in unnatural ways, almost like video imaging, it truly is hard to look at. Up to this point in my life, most visions would go just as fast as they came. My ability was in a snapshot of time, two to three seconds. These visions, however, were longer, and I literally had to open my eyes for them to stop because I could not bear the sight. I was, for the first time in my life, deathly scared of something. Previously when I saw demonic beings, I was not scared; I would get angry. This, however, felt different and looked different than anything I had dealt with before. I was afraid.

I sat straight up in my bed and replayed what had taken place in my mind, trying to figure out what in the world was going on. About five minutes went by, and I got the strength to try once again to get comfortable and sleep. I didn't want to. I was freaked out, but I had to try. I shut my eyes, and within a split second, a larger figure emerged that was hefty in size. He was completely dirty, bald, and eating furiously. This figure was eating like a wolf or wild animal would devour its prey. He was ravaging uncooked meat, gnawing his own arm, and tearing off his flesh like an insane animal. It was disgusting! Blood was running down his face and body, and he was eating so fast it would make anyone sick to watch. He was violently twerking his head and body as if he was having seizures while eating.

I started crying out of pure fear. Imagine a six-foot, 225-pound, thirty-three-year-old man literally crying out of fear in his bed like a child. The first thing that came to mind was my trip to that stupid pagan healing store earlier that day! "I knew I shouldn't have gone there!" I cried. I prayed and repented with everything I had, wailing like a baby, asking God to please, please forgive me. I laid it all out to Christ, my hope and faith totally resting with Him.

I did not want to wake my wife and scare or worry her, so I tried to be as quiet as I possibly could. The entire bed was shaking and drenched with sweat due to my fear. I don't know how she didn't wake up. It *had* to have been the Lord's doing. I must have prayed for ten minutes, apologizing for going to that place, knowing how many times the Bible says to not consult mediums, sorcerers, or healers. I poured out my heart to God with everything I could think of that I had done wrong in my life. Never in my existence have I ever been so afraid. I prayed for my life to be saved. I thought maybe this was it; I was about to die or truly get possessed by demons or something. All the while tears were rolling down my face. Finally, I rolled over in bed after I had prayed for what seemed like forever.

Suddenly, three men dressed in ancient armor from head to toe, riding horses with armor, descended upon me. The middle warrior looked me straight in the eye with a confident smirk on his face. As they came closer, I could see their faces; they were in human form with beards, and they all wore helmets. The one in the middle had longer brown hair, and he nodded his head to me as if to say, "What's up?" or "I got this." It was as if he knew me or that we knew each other. My first reaction was fear. I knew that I would not be able to handle these three men. Then the most incredible thing happened within seconds of watching them descend. Tears of terror instantly became tears of joy. A sudden peace and joy came over me; I was crying in amazement. Peace and comfort that could only come from God and Angels of the Lord was with them.

As my emotions did a complete 180, I saw flashes of light throughout my bedroom and down the hallway. A battle inside my house began between these warriors of God and evil spirits, and it took place right before my eyes. The lights were like fireflies flying around the room, flashing every few seconds. I had this unbelievable feeling that I can only describe as heavenly. I went to my knees. I knew right there and then, at that very moment, that everything was going to be OK. It was like the Holy Spirit was filling me. Nothing had to be said or explained; I just knew exactly what was going on. These warriors came by order of God to fight these demons and redeem my soul. The Lord heard my prayer.

It's difficult to explain the roller-coaster ride of emotions, but it might be as if someone close to you had drowned and then a few minutes later was resuscitated, and the feeling you would get once your friend or family member was alive again. It was that type of extreme emotions. The only difference is that it was supernatural. I was so pumped up and overjoyed that I literally ran down the hallway to the family room and started fist pumping and screaming in a whisper, trying not to wake up my family. I could not go back to sleep the rest of the night. These flashes around my home lasted over three hours. I was overwhelmed by the Spirit and constantly kept praising God and going to my knees. I watched TV in the living room, seeing these firefly-like flashes every ten seconds or so. Even as I ate a bowl of cereal a couple hours later, they were lighting up all over the house—in the kitchen, in my other family room. It was crazy but awesome.

I truly do not know what would have happened if they had not come. One thing is for sure, and there's not a doubt in my mind: these warriors from God saved me. I have no idea why this happened or why Christ decided to save a scumbag like me, but He did, and I love Him for that. I will always be in debt to Him. What's even more amazing is that God loves His children more than we could ever love Him in our sinful bodies, which is awesome. He will never give up on you if you believe. I was redeemed.

That night changed my life forever. I have never touched cocaine or looked at pornography since. Not once! That's how powerful the Lord and His Angels are. Both of those addictions were history in a twinkling of an eye without any withdrawals whatsoever! I was instantly cleansed of both addictions and never had the urge to do cocaine again.

I wrote everything that happened to me down that night. Incredibly, what took place afterward was amazing as well. My ability or vision—glimpses of time, people, and dreams—had become much more understandable. I no longer only saw faces; I was seeing objects and other forms of communication with more clarity in my visions. I had a sense of understanding and purpose, and I had become more aware of my surroundings. I still get chills up and down my spine just thinking about it. Why God saved me I have no idea. I'm not worthy of Him, and I have sinned and made mistakes just as much if not more than the next man, but He still loves me as His son. He still took me in and held me close.

If you don't believe God can forgive *any* sins you may have committed, you are wrong! Look at what a piece of garbage I was. He still took me in. Jesus takes all comers. It doesn't matter what you have done. If you believe, repent, and call upon Christ's name, He will come to you and deliver. The Apostle Paul was one of the Jewish Pharisees who persecuted the early Christians and sentenced them to death before Jesus appeared to him and blinded him for three days (Acts 9). Paul was a murderer. Christ still took him. King David, son of Jesse, the second king of Israel, committed adultery and then had his mistress's husband killed in battle (2 Sam. 11). God still forgave him. Last but not least, Jacob, son of Isaac, betrayed his older brother, Esau, and deceived his father for essentially the birthrights and blessings of the family (Gen. 27). God changed Jacob's name to Israel. He forgives! He can change your life! He loves you! Jesus doesn't care what you did in the past; He cares about your future with Him!

> He is the Great Redeemer.
> He is Emmanuel—God is with us.
> He is the divine Lamb.
> He is the Prince of Peace.
> The Son of God.
> The Great Shepherd.
> The Conqueror.
> He is the King.
> He is the Lion of the tribe of Judah.
> He is the Savior, the Way, and the Light.
> "No man comes to the Father but through Jesus Christ!"
> (John 14:6)
> Praise the Lord! Accept Him and rejoice
> and He will give you the keys to the Kingdom
> of Heaven!

August 4, 2014

Now I knew this was for real, but I wasn't out of the woods yet. I was still confused about what took place, and honestly, the angelic warriors motivated me to a higher level to kill evil and destroy the wicked. (I know, I'm weird and borderline psycho lol.) But after seeing a flat-out spiritual battle in my home, that's exactly what I wanted to do in the physical realm. Not the common sin we commit every day but the next level of sinners: those who bring others down, poison society, and steal wages; the ones who spread their cancer and self-indulge in sin. These were the marked ones I wanted to destroy in every way. I wanted not only to kill these evil men but to erase their entire existence forever. This is how angry I was at the unrighteous. This was the last stronghold that our adversary had on me.

Hate! Hate is a terrible sin. Hate can make people do or say something they regret for a lifetime. They say there is a thin line between love and hate. Absolutely there is. You cannot hate unless you have loved. I used to be exactly who I hated. I loved doing evil for a while, and my love turned to hate. So as this hatred spread through my soul, I began getting ready for war. I had gotten the wrong impression of these Angels coming into my home at first. I was incredibly encouraged, fired up, and ready for battle.

It was Monday morning, four days after God had sent His mighty warriors. I had loaded my twelve-gauge and my Sig .380, with fifteen rounds in each mag. My Glock 9mm inside my belt. I had my knife strapped to my leg, along with another on my side. The ammo box was full in the trunk of my car. I was ready. I had to drop off my kids at day camp and stop by the bank before I headed down to the spot. I did not care about any of the people I would retaliate against or the family and friends I would affect by my decision. I was just stone-cold ready for war. I accepted the fact that if I killed one person and then died or went to jail, I would have made the world a better place. After all, in my mind I was working for the Lord, doing His dirty work. Why else could I see this spiritual world beyond our understanding, I thought, plus see a flat-out spiritual battle right before my eyes?

I dropped off my kids and went to the bank. I pulled in the parking lot, headed toward the door, walked in, stood in line, and waited my turn. I had to take care of some bills before my two kids and I went to visit my parents down south. I would raid these houses and scurry out of town the next morning. This would give me time to reflect and build a stronger sense of what took place, along with not being in the state just in case something went array. I was pumped up and mentally prepared. The bank was four miles north of where my escapade would begin.

As I was standing in line at the bank, maybe about one or two minutes, a hand landed on my shoulder. I turned around and could not believe my eyes. There standing in front of me, was the pastor of the church I attended and grew up in until I went to college. I had not seen this man in fifteen years. It was unreal; I felt as if I was in some slow-motion trance. We shook hands and gave each other a hug, but all I could get out of my mouth was "Wow, the Lord works in mysterious ways!" I was completely dumbfounded, but I gathered up enough strength to tell him I wanted to talk to him outside. I was so scatterbrained that I had walked away without taking the $2,500

I had withdrawn from the bank teller! I left it sitting on the counter, and she had to call me back to retrieve it.

I waited outside the bank until Pastor was done so we could talk and catch up. As I waited by my car for him to come out, I could barely think straight. I was in such shock. I knew this was a sign from God. The chances of me running into my old pastor after fifteen years—on this exact day, at this exact time, and right before I was going to commit murder and raid a drug house—was not a coincidence. Not after I had witnessed the Lord's Angels visit my home four days earlier.

Pastor finally came out, and we started talking. The first thing he said was "Man, my wife made a huge breakfast this morning, and I never leave the house without eating breakfast, but the Lord told me I had to go to the bank at ten o'clock this morning, and not a minute later. My wife made a good breakfast today too!" We laughed about him not eating, and he asked how I was doing. I believe I had a lot more to say than what he bargained for that Monday morning. I unloaded on him. I did not tell him what my full intentions were, but I gave him the gist of what had been happening to me for the past year and a half of my life. I told him certain things I had been seeing, as well as the visions. I was so amazed that he was at the bank at this exact time that I just started opening up about everything I had kept inside. It was pretty deep stuff to tell someone you haven't seen in fifteen years.

My lips were quivering like a young child as I tried to hold back my tears and talk as best I could. He was amazed and seemed to believe me, but I'm sure it was a little overwhelming to him. He probably thought I was having a breakdown or something. However, he did not know the extent of what had been going on in my life and that God was working through him at that exact moment to send a message to me. Nevertheless, we talked a little more and I asked about his two sons, who were roughly the same age as me. I had attended youth group with them. While we were talking, he looked down at his watch and said, "It has been forty years since I was saved; today is my birthday!" He was referring to being born again. He looked at his watch again and said, "You know what? This is weird, but it's the exact time of day I was all messed up on methadone when I walked off the street and into that church, which changed my life forever." For me, it was one of those *aha* moments where the lightbulb goes off in your head.

There was no way of denying God's power and presence that morning. It was by the grace and blessing of God that this happened. Once again, the Lord sent a messenger to me in the form of my old pastor, and saved me from destruction. Twice in four days! Pastor proceeded to tell me that maybe I needed to rely on Jesus more and that God loved me. Maybe God was trying to tell me to make an effort to change other people's hearts and that this was happening for a reason and not some random experience. He also invited me to his Bible study on Tuesday nights. We talked for a few more minutes, hugged each other, prayed together, and went our separate ways.

This experience was deeply moving to me, and I realized what God was trying to tell me. The Holy Spirit filled me with love. I was ecstatic and stopped at a gas station down the street to compose myself. After a few minutes of praying, repenting, and thanking the Lord, I called my mother who had told me a few months ago that maybe I should give our old pastor a call. I had briefly told her some of the experiences that had been going on supernaturally in my life over the past year. She was surprised yet understanding. She was glad I had connected with our old pastor, even if it was for only a few minutes, but she encouraged me to join the Bible study he had invited me to attend. After repenting right there at the gas station, I headed back home and never looked back. My days of revenge and being a mercenary for justice were over.

Now I had received the sign that I had been waiting months for! It was quite clear. *Love,* not war. And one absolute fact: God is in control and still on the throne. He will protect His own and He will never forsake them. It is a wonderful and humbling feeling to know that, without a doubt, Christ loves you, especially when you do not deserve it. What a wonderful family to be in, a heavenly family that looks out for each and every creation that belongs to God. We are all so blessed to have a Father who loves us like He does.

As I recap and write this testimony about what took place, throwing myself under the bus completely and exposing all of the negative, horrible secrets of the last few years of my life, which is insane. I know that nobody will look at me the same after they have read this. I know that my life will change forever. I also know God is molding me for what will happen after I release this story. There will be many who line up to mock and discount some of the truth of this testimony and the messages of warning I received from Christ. Lord Jesus will seek out the ones who need this story and fulfill whatever His will is for my testimony. My faith is strong now, and I know I'm on the correct path. It is in God's hands, and I wouldn't want it any other way. Paul teaches us, "Be honest in your evaluation of yourselves, measure yourselves by how much faith God has given you" (Rom. 12:3).

I have received heavenly signs and messages, so my test of faith is clear. I have to do this for you, and to glorify the Lord God Almighty. I have been rapidly advancing into this spiritual world. I know why this is happening. I am so excited that I can barely sit still, waiting for the next chapter in my life. Also, I now know that whatever and wherever the next chapter of my life leads, will completely depend on Christ and allow Him to guide my feet in everything I do.

Over the course of four days, two major turning points in my life had taken place. After that Monday morning when I saw Pastor at the bank, I repented and finally got the picture. I knew I was meant to serve Jesus Christ, and I made a commitment to Him that day to work for the Lord the rest of my life. His will could take over my life and I would do my humanly best to please, honor, and glorify Him.

Praise be to the Father!
Praise be to our King, Jesus Christ!
Praise and hallelujah be to the Holy Spirit that Christ sent after victory on the cross!

The Spirit of the Lord and His Call

August 5, 2014

The Spirit of the Lord came upon me, giving instructions and calling me into service.

After running into my old pastor on Monday, I left that following morning with my children to visit my parents and grandparents who live in the South. I felt the Holy Spirit churning within me at a constant rate after a couple hours of driving. My thoughts were not of this world, and I broke down in tears of joy and amazement during the first couple hours of the trip. I kept wondering what was wrong with me and was desperately trying to conceal my emotions, so I would not wake up my children. Luckily, they slept most of the morning because we had left at 4:00 a.m. It's a good ten-hour trip to my parents' house. I like to get started early so we have a little time in the afternoon to enjoy ourselves, instead of wasting the entire day driving. Mainly I like to leave early so my kids will sleep a few hours and I will have a peaceful car ride during the morning. We all know how six- and seven-year-olds get on long car rides.

I had been going through extreme emotions for about two hours. At one point I truly thought I was dying, but I cannot fully explain the feeling. The love and power of this feeling was so great that I thought maybe this was it: God was taking me home. I even asked the Lord out loud if I was dying! The pure glory of our Lord God truly puts in perspective how completely unworthy and dependent upon Him we really are. This glory proves the fact that our earthly body could never handle Heaven or the full presence of our Holy Lord. Then, just before I was about to stop for breakfast, the Spirit of the Lord came upon me. Suddenly I had this incredible urge to write in the notebook on my phone app. There were two things I was told to write down:

1. Write a book.
2. A full-page sermon or speech on becoming a true Christian spiritually.

I probably wrote a full page and a half sermon, typing and crying uncontrollably. It was as if I was not in control of my writing. I was compelled and commanded to do so. My children were fast asleep while this was going on. It seemed during the pouring out of my emotions, God made sure my children remained asleep and that I received His message. I was thinking, talking, and writing in ways I had never thought of before. Nothing other than the Holy Spirit can do such things. Directly after I wrote this on my iPhone, two semi-trucks appeared coming down the freeway ramp next to me. Both had huge crosses on the backs of their trailers, with the words "Life Way Christian Publishing" underneath them.

It was totally out of this world. For the first time in my life, I felt that right there, at that specific moment in time, I was exactly where I was supposed to be in this world, writing the instructions I had been given in my notepad.

When we arrived at my mother's house, I briefly told her what had happened during the car ride but did not get into specifics. We had a great time throughout the week, and I knew, for some reason unknown to me, that instead of leaving early Sunday morning to go back home, I had to stay one extra day so I could go to church with my parents. I had this deep feeling of, I *must* go to church Sunday morning. So all week I kept arguing with my wife on the phone about when I would be coming home. I kept telling her, "I can't come home on Sunday; I have to come home on Monday instead. I don't know why, I just have to go to church on Sunday morning with my parents." She wasn't happy because we had plans for Sunday when I returned and didn't understand. At any rate, I decided to stay an extra day.

August 10, 2014

On Sunday morning, the Spirit of the Lord came upon me again. I had the sudden urge to rewrite, on paper, the speech I had wrote earlier that week in the car. At the top of this paper, I was told to write a scripture from the prophet Joel:

"And it shall come to pass afterward, that I will pour out My Spirit upon all flesh; and your sons and your daughters shall prophesy, your old men shall dream dreams, your young men shall see visions" (Joel 2:28).

My mother was wondering why I was writing on paper, using the Bible as my reference. At first, I did not want to tell her what I had been feeling, but she was persistent so I told her. "I know exactly what the pastor is going to preach about today. I wrote notes on the drive here, and for some reason, I have to rewrite it on this piece of paper and give it to your pastor after the service." She looked at me as if I was crazy, just like any normal person would if he or she heard such things. Then she said, "Umm, OK." And gave me a look that said, "You are mentally disabled," and walked away. I'm sure most of you know that look. So as we drove to her church, I held my Bible with the speech inside.

We arrived at church and greeted everyone. I knew a few people at my mother's church down south because I had attended it quite often when I lived there and went to college in the state. The service started with music and songs for everyone as churches normally do. At this particular church, the pastor and his family were musically oriented. Each family member played a different instrument—guitar, piano, drums, and voice. It was cool, and the common man was made to feel comfortable. It's a come-as-you-are, Bible-based church, any and all welcome.

The preacher began the service with his planned sermon, but roughly at the halfway point, *it* happened. He plainly said, "I don't know why, but I have to stop my sermon and talk about this." That's when, for the next five minutes, the pastor preached basically everything I had written down earlier that week. For the first couple of paragraphs, he used what I wrote almost word for word. I was rocking in my chair with amazement and unbelief! I kept looking over at my parents saying, "Wow" and "I told you, I told you!"

It was a moving service with passion and fire. I believe three or four people went up to the altar and gave their lives to Jesus that morning. While the last few minutes of service were wrapping up, I handed my iPhone to my mother so she could see the notes I had written on the way to her house earlier that week. She looked at me, and after the first few sentences, she gave me the *Twilight Zone*, eyes-wide-open look.

After the service was over, I got up and handed what I had written on paper to the pastor. It was an amazing experience only God could make happen. I told him how the notes had transpired and that it was almost exactly what he preached about through the last half of service. All the while I was trying my best to compose myself without balling like a baby. Since then we have kept in touch, and the preacher along with his assistant have been very supportive, especially through my advancement into demonic warfare.

I never cry, barely ever. But since all this has taken place, I find myself so emotional that I can barely control it sometimes. It must be the pure love I feel. The Holy Spirit is the greatest gift anyone can ever receive. I was on fire for the Lord after the service. My mother and aunt told me that what took place was a confirmation from God that the message and instructions I had received and wrote earlier that week were from the Lord. The first words I wrote on that Tuesday morning were "write a book." So that is why I am writing this testimony for you, my friends, and to bring glory to the Father.

The second message I wrote on Tuesday, August 5th was:

Open up your Spirit and Soul

To become a Christian, a true Christian, you must empty your heart, soul, spirit, and everything you've got into Jesus Christ. It's not just saying the words or methodically going to the preacher or priest and repeating what is said. It is a complete surrender of yourself, knowing what a sinner you are and accepting Christ as the Son of God. This isn't some ritual that takes place; this must be between you and Jesus. There is no other mediator between you and the Father. He is the way the truth, and the life. You must open your spirit to Him, pass that comfort zone, and go all the way, totally submitting yourself to Christ. You must believe with all of your soul, 100 percent, and without a doubt that He came to Earth as the Son of God, died on the cross for the sins of mankind, and was resurrected three days later, defeating death and entering the Kingdom of Heaven. You must believe He was the total sacrifice, that Christ laid His life down for us, and came to Earth as a servant of the Lord, so all who believe in Him may not perish but have everlasting life. This must come from deep within you, from the bottom of your heart, as you confess that Jesus is Lord, repent of your sins, and most of all truly love Jesus

Christ for who He is and what He has done for you.

Love is the key! Love of the Father! Love of Christ and love of one another!

Love breaks down walls! Love is everything! Nothing can stop love!

Nothing can get in the way of someone who is compelled by total love.

Love is stronger than anything evil can throw at us!

Love *is* and always will be all you need!

Love will open doors! Love will allow you to see who you really are!

Love cuts like a double-edged sword!

God is love and His love for us is infinite!

Praise Jesus! He did everything for love, and we owe Him everything!

Love Him back! Accept Him! He is worthy of our praise!

In eleven days, my life was literally turned upside down, a complete 180 degrees. Christ had redeemed and plucked me out of sure disaster. I should be in jail, dead, or in a strait jacket. He apparently has other plans for me. When God is ready to move, nothing on this Earth or in the universe can stop Him.

September 2014

I was still addicted to Suboxone, which, if you remember, is used to treat narcotic (opiate) addictions, plus I was smoking two packs of cigarettes a day. God helped me wrestle away my Suboxone/pain medication addiction, and finally. . . finally. . . I was free of that stranglehold on my life, which had been with me for over four years! I couldn't move for almost two weeks from the withdrawals. I quit cold turkey, but I made it through by holding on to Christ's feet every step of the way like a child who holds a father's leg, begging Him not to leave. Every test and trial you endure will slowly make you stronger, and your faith in God will grow more and more.

One month later, in October, God started knocking at my door about smoking. I tell you, I argued with Him for a few weeks on this issue. I loved smoking, and I wasn't going to quit, no way, no how. I pleaded my case with God saying, "You have taken all my other addictions away. Can't I just do one thing that I like? Look what I have been through in such a short period of time! This is asking too much. All I want to do is smoke, and I like doing it. No way, I can't quit smoking right now. I need to smoke, and I'm not open to the thought of even trying to quit."

During this period, I had begun the battle against familiar spirits and distinguishing them. Discernment of spirits is one of the gifts of the Holy Spirit that Paul talks about in 1 Corinthians 12—spiritual discernment between good and evil spirits, as well as between messages, dreams, and visions, whether they come from the Lord or something malevolent. This is a continual battle that never ends for a seer of the Lord. As I said before, there is a spiritual war going on relentlessly behind the scenes that is setting the stage for the ultimate showdown.

Nevertheless, God imposed His will upon me and sent a spirit of pride to wrestle me. I had to do my first extensive study and research on the Book of Job to understand what and who I was fighting. Those who are wise understand: Only God can reveal your pride and draw out the spirit of leviathan through prayer and fasting. In my case, He showed my pride in smoking. My final smoke was on October 31, 2014. And within three months, from July 31 to October 31, Christ had taken away all my addictions: cocaine, drinking, Suboxone, prescription pain drugs, pornography, and smoking. Three months! Only through Christ is that possible! "I can do all things through Christ who strengthens me" (Phil. 4:13).

God left me with only one addiction: Him.

Christ will never give up on you. Don't believe Satan. You can do it! Through Christ all things are possible, just believe and have faith. Don't listen to those demons that torment you. Victory can be won through Jesus. You will receive power when the Holy Spirit comes upon you. You can disarm the powers of Satan by believing in Christ and accepting Him as the Son of God. Take control of your life for the first time and *believe*!

Say it:

I am a child of God! I am a child of God! Christ is my savior!

C'mon, what are you waiting for?

Take His hand; He will never give up on you.

We need you! Lie down and submit to Him.

He will give you eternal life in Heaven. He is the only way!

Jesus Christ is the name.

Chant His name: Jesus Christ! Jesus Christ! Jesus Christ!

From August 2013 through May of 2017, I had only worked a total of six months. I did not understand why the Lord would not allow me to have a job until recently. Even when I tried, it was like my mind was elsewhere, and I had no drive or strength to work. You know that I have two children and a wife, who has worked her hands to the bone, supporting us during all of this. It breaks my heart, knowing what she has gone through. She has been doing the Lord's work by supporting me and our children financially, as well as giving our Lord Jesus time to groom and polish me for the service that has been given to me. I pray God reveals that truth to my wife.

Our Lord asked me, "Did I not send My Apostle Paul off for three years in order to train him? Have I not trained and groomed My other children, whom I chose for specific duties?" I could only bow my head and accept what He was doing in my life. I owe Christ everything. I know all of this was and is for Him. I owe my life to Him. I want all this to be for God's glory and to save as many lives as possible through Christ Jesus, my King. I will become a soldier for the Kingdom of Heaven, for Father God Almighty, for all my Holy family in the heavenly kingdoms! In Jesus Christ's name we will be victorious!

So I tell you this not from my own words but from the Lord Christ Himself. It is the polishing of the gold that brings out the shine. When He decides to mold you, it is for His glory and a blessing for you and all to receive.

Since the day of my calling from the Lord, I have faced great persecution, trials, and tests of my faith. I am going through the gauntlet with familiar spirits, demonic forces, and principalities in the heavenly realms unimaginable to the common man. Many things must remain secret, for my King and Savior, Christ Jesus, has told me repeatedly not to go into detail about what has taken place so that I do not get puffed up with pride. I have given up everything for the task Christ has given to me. I have sacrificed all I have to write this book. I have laid it all out on the line. I can barely pay my bills and am flat broke, but for Jesus I will do anything. This is bigger than you or me. This is eternity! And Christ is my Lord, whom I will lay my life down for. My hope and faith totally rest in Him. How wonderful He is. O, Lord Jesus, this is for you and for the people this will save. I love you with everything I have! I give all of myself to you, my King!

As any good student and servant of the Lord would do, I began to study the Word of God intensely. It was a burning passion and desire from the Holy Spirit inside me. It has become an obsession really. I study the Word every free second I have. I have no job, other than to allow the Holy Spirit to teach and counsel me. I cannot seem to focus on anything other than Christ and wisdom. The Lord gave me teachers of the Word, when He needed to, through His servants. Since we live in the age of great knowledge where information is just a click away, as our brother Daniel prophesied, I was on the Internet constantly, studying until I went to bed. I compared notes in my Bible and learned about geography, theology, discernment, spiritual warfare, and whatever else God guided me to in order to grow in wisdom. I am not stretching the truth when I say that the Lord Jesus wrote this book through me and personally guided and taught me.

This all led up to the time when God would instruct me to become a watchman. To send His message of warning of the coming judgment, and to inspire my brothers and sisters in Christ to become warriors in the Lord of Heaven's Armies. And now is the time!

THE PROPHETIC BOOKS OF JOSHUA DAVID

I Joshua David

A Prayer for America

O, Lord Most High, savior of the Gentiles, who created this great nation. I beg of you on behalf of our people and those who do not know you, to please be merciful. I know your wrath, and I know what you can do. But please remember how we were founded upon you, O Lord. You nurtured her and fed her and allowed her to grow to heights never before seen on this planet. You made her the pinnacle of the world, a model of what a nation should be under God. Remember how she was your right hand of judgment to the rest of the nations. I beg you to remember how you struck fear in enemy nations' hearts and used her to show grace and love in many humanitarian efforts around the globe. Remember how she protected and loved Israel, her sister, for so long, as you loved her.

We in North America loved you at one time with all of our hearts, Father. Remember how we would send our missionaries for you, Lord? We have reached the ends of the Earth for you, Lord Jesus. For we have a fallen nature, which we cannot hide from. Your judgment is just. We have defiled ourselves and followed the world, walking away from our foundation in you, Lord.

I beg you, please be merciful and protect your Saints as you swing the sickle upon us. We have many true Saints on her lands, and we are the Nation of the Cross. Remember that, Father. We have slapped you in the face and turned from the One who gave us glory, honor, and respect. And now we have become what is mocked and hated throughout the world, even though no other nation in history has been more generous as we have. I plead that you find a way of escape for many, so we can regroup and rejoice in your name once again. I know we must sit back and watch how other nations will consume your first love, but remember how you loved us too. We protected Israel in your name, helping her become a nation once again. We responded during the last judgment you gave us during the Great Depression seventy years ago and turned the tide for your people in that great war. I know your seventy-year blessing is over now. Please allow your Saints to stay strong and stand fast as we hold on until we can be caught up with you. We will wait for you, O Lord, and we love you. Remember us.

America's Judgment Announced

The Spirit of the Lord came upon me on September 4, 2015, during the reign of President Barrack Obama's 7th year saying: "Give this message to America." I could barely move for two days as I fasted and fought within myself for being unworthy to relay and write these messages.

This is what the Lord says:

"You have walked away from Me. Fallen are you. There is no turning back now—only judgment awaits. That bull will go down, see your futures and finances crash. Who will comfort you? Who will you plead and beg for? I will say, "Who is this that comes too late? I do not know you." Strap the ram's horn to your mouth! Let nothing come between the air you breathe and the horn. Walk day and night sounding the alarm. That disgusting and abominable statue off the coast of the city that never sleeps will be destroyed and underwater. She has been a whore. She turned you to worship her freedom. Freedom from Me! You slept with her finances, you whored with her sexual immorality, and you committed adultery with other nations as you turned your back on My Jacob. The one you swore to protect forever! You leave Me little choice, as if I had one.

"I gave you *warnings* recently, but you are blinded by your self-indulgence and vanity. Now you will mourn for your country. Flee for the hills; flee for the mountains. You have betrayed the Lord your God after everything I have done for you. No longer will the nations fear you. No longer will they take your word to heart. Your pride will be shattered. You are a prideful nation that expects much for very little. The nations will laugh at you. They will say, 'Remember how great that nation was? Now look at it.' You will become a mockery for the drunkards in other nations. Your apostasy has come to Me like a boiling pot, overflowing, burning everything in its path. Watch how I break your strongholds. You think you have financial problems now? Wait till I have backhanded you, you arrogant, disobedient children. Stretch your arms out in wonder, wail on the streets, and weep for yourselves. Who will you call on now? I made you. You were My gem. I loved you and nourished you. I would have had all nations bow to you as My right hand. I am coming against you. You will know who I am once again. You provoked Me to anger. Now the time of the end must come; it is upon you now.

I, the Lord God of Israel, have spoken!"

"You say, 'Why teach our children the good news?' Now your children will grow up blinded, and I will send them into the pit!

"You say, 'We are the trading capital of the world.' Now your ports will be smashed, and the value of your gold decimated.

"You say, 'How great the city of New York is; we will take refuge there.' I will completely destroy New York, it is filled with every lust imaginable to this world.

"You say, 'We are too strong, nothing can stop us.' Now one of your legs will be amputated for the nations to watch you hobble around. You will be the beggar instead of the borrower. Prepare for the great famine I am sending forth. I will cause food to be so scarce many will ponder eating their own children. Get ready! The scales will have no food in them to measure."

A Call to Repentance

"Come to Me now! You want to know if I am merciful? Come quick because I have cut time short. Lay your heads down and cry out to Me, raise your hands in surrender once again. I will love you like My child once again. Lay down your apostasy and come back to Me. Mammon will not save you! Only I can. I will open My arms to you in comfort, so you will endure. I will cradle you until I call you home. Put on your sack cloth and repent. Tell Me that you love Me. Tell Me you are sorry. Tell Me how you need Me, and I will be there with you. You have read My promises—that I will save My people from the time of testing. You must return at once! There was a time when we walked together. Come back. My hand is out."

To the Southern Kingdom

This is what the Lord says:

"I expected more out of you in the Southern States; your young have started drifting. You are My heart, My belt, and My Judah. Act like it! I know how you kept My Word close through this terrible time. Tell your children to return. You know the way, guide them. I will give peace to those who come in time of trouble. Neighboring nations will still pay attention to how you react, so set an example. Get ready because I am moving swiftly! The light stand must be turned on and tended. Do not let it out! Let it be known that I am the Lord your God.

I, Jesus Christ the Mighty, have spoken!"

What the Lord has Against North America

"Your political scene is an absolute disaster. Your leaders are as worthless and untrustworthy as the donkey. Does anyone tell the truth? Lies, slander, and discord are all you know. To make matters worse, all of you play the prostitute, sexually and morally, and are drunkards. You dine with the enemy and drink to prosperity and wealth. Afterward, when you are done treating your enemies like royalty, they scheme behind your back, plot destruction and publicly shame you in front of the other nations. You have grown so weak that you laugh with them, showing what lack of confidence you really have, but you are so arrogant that you notice not. All you have left is boastful pride, swallowing like a pig in your glory days. So as the leaders go, so do My people.

"Sexual immorality of the grossest kind is taking place among My people. It is like a never-ending whorehouse for the younger generation. You have led them into the most severe harlotry possible and are to blame for their fall. Even the men act like prostitutes. Where has the man of the household gone? Even he lies next to his brother, and their wives lie next to each other, gorging on their lust for one another. I am against you for this! Know that! You have run with weakness in your eyes, begging for help from China instead of Me. You look to other immoral nations for help, and lie in bed with them, giving yourself to them freely. You beg other nations like a whore who doesn't care if she receives payment or not. Now who rules over you with their fists?

"All you had to do was come to Me for everything you needed. You do not listen, nor care to even look back at Me when I give My mighty Angels the order to lift your protection and chastise you. You do not even take time to hear the messages and warnings I have given to My servants, shepherds, and prophets. You are too busy with all of your possessions, wealth and making sure you look good to others. You want everyone to envy you? I will take that away first. No nation will envy you but will look down upon you! I gave a similar message to My prophets during the Assyrian invasion, and now I must give this message again. It is too late; I must forgo judgment upon you. At least in ages past, people still went to My houses of worship. The apostasy in your lands has reached to the Heavens; the stench of the West Coast has reached even to Me. A storm is coming; see the people run for their lives on the sands of the seashore. Watch how the homes and bodies stack up. The stench will get much worse! You have been so spoiled that you will live in shock and despair, and mourn for yourselves continually. Those who are My people will finally have the light go off inside their stubborn heads. They will come back to Me, and I will once again call them My children.

"As for My Holy people of Israel, whom My first covenant is with, I tell you: go back now! Head to your land I have promised; only there can I protect you. This includes those who live in Europe. Go to the land of Jacob, where I will wrestle you as I wrestled him in the wilderness. You will call Me God and Messiah. I will break your leg, Israel, and then you will know 'Yeshua is Lord' when I have My vengeance upon the nations!!

This is the command given to you by the Most High, God of Abraham!"

America the Unfaithful

Again, the Spirit of the Lord came unto Joshua saying, "Give this message."

This is what the Lord says:

"As if prostituting yourself wasn't enough, the most abominable of acts are taking place and have been for quite some time. You have been sacrificing your own children, not on altars or to foreign gods, but much worse. You sacrifice your own children to yourself, out of total selfishness, inconvenience, and complete dismissal of responsibility. Such things are unheard of. Not even Israel, in its darkest days of idolatry, killed its children for selfish and prideful ambitions. At least they were led astray by false prophets and the evil rulers of the atmospheric realm. You are children of pride! What arrogance to kill an unborn child before it even comes out of the womb, simply because it doesn't fit in with the life you lead. Who has told you to do such things? Spilling of innocent blood is one of the things I hate most, yet you continue to slaughter My infant children. Who are you to decide what life to take before it even begins? I have prepared a special place for all who do these things, without complete repentance and mourning to Me. They will be chained down in Tartarus for these acts, until the Lake of Fire has been prepared.

"Do you not know that I created all life and cultivate each person in the womb of his or her mother? I give the spirit of life inside of the womb, only to have the spirit come right back to Me after My child has been brutally murdered because of a darkened heart of pride and ambitious motives. You, America, were My gem! Why have you forsaken Me in this way? Why? I loved you and you left Me. Why? O how I rage with anger!"

A Message to Canada

Again, the Lord said unto Joshua, "Prophesy against Canada."

This is what the Lord says:

"Do not think this judgment will pass you by. O Canada, you and the States are like sisters with the same blood. You ride the coattails of your big sister— as she goes, so do you. What is good for her is good for you, so what judgments come to her will be yours too. I see the same heart between both of you. You are inseparable, joined by the hip. Therefore, your ways have mimicked your sister's, and for that I find you guilty of the same crimes. In fact, your law on marriage set the precedent. Restore what faith you still have and repent. I will be there to comfort you through the terrible times headed your way. Remember that I will chastise My children and ones whom I love to prepare them for what is about to come, so be ready for when I do. Come to Me like children running to the safety of their Father's arms, and I will make sure to give you peace and salvation. I will call you My own once again."

A Message to Mexico

The Lord said, "Send this message to your neighbor on the Southern border."

This is what the Lord Almighty says:

"Have you not seen or felt the constant judgment to your country? Your land has been cursed from the beginning. Complete unrest and times of calamity have always been with you! For centuries innocent blood was shed on your lands and has ruined the earth. Where you reside is like Satan's playground of the West. Anything goes; corruption to the highest degree, murder and prostitution, and making children harlots is your forte. Strong drink and drugs have decayed the foundation of the land. You have tried to escape your own lands from the beginning, and now I am moving a great multitude to the North. I say unto you, come back to Me, and truly speak and repent to the Lord your God. Do not run to your emblems, statues, priests, and figures to worship. Sit down and talk to *Me*! I am your Lord, Jesus Christ! Come to Me personally, and I will comfort you and have fellowship. Too long have I watched you play the harlot in Thyatira, when each and every one of you can go directly to Me for everything. Put away your statues and rosaries! Just raise your arms to Me and speak your heart. I am with you! Repent and ask Me to guide and give you rest, and it will-be-done. For many of you, things cannot get much worse, so hold on just a little while longer, for I am coming soon.

I, the Lord of Salvation and Redemption, have spoken!"

Woe to the Wealthy

"You say you are untouchable, residing in all of your winter cottages and summer homes. Those will be gone *first!* Your great stonework with granite and marble—everything will be lost. You lounge in luxury and prosperity, indulging yourselves with everything you desire, and give no thanks to Me! You buy only the choicest meats, finest wines, and most expensive fragrances and oils just to pamper yourselves and boast to others. Hear this and listen well! Slowly I will take away all those things. Like a vise I will continue to squeeze you. Every time you think that things will get better, I will squeeze you again. Sell, sell, and lose, lose all your possessions! A slow death to all your fine things! When you say, 'This must be it; surely things cannot get any worse,' that is when I will crank the vise again. I will turn you into what you laugh at and look down upon. It will be like walking in a swamp. Every time you wiggle your foot out of the muck, it will step right back into the slop and dig in, further than before. And it will not end! Finally, after I have squeezed every drop out of you, many will see again and not be blinded. Pray that it will be before the time of the end."

A Feast for My Remnant

O Israel, how I have missed you so much! You do not realize how long I have waited this very moment. To once again call you children of God. My sons and My daughters what tremendous Jubilee we will have. When I return, we will set up the Kingdom, and you will be My heart once again. I have missed you like a soldier misses his wife during a long war. I cannot wait to hold you in My arms once again with the festival trumpets blowing and the wine flowing. Great sweet and savory we will partake together. The Heavens will all come in for the Feast. Your sisters and brothers of past will join. My Holy Seraphim, Cherubim, and all Holy creations will sit in honor with you at the table, as we all are together at last. We will be in such joy. On that day, no work will be required of anyone. All will help with the feast. It will be a thanksgiving of tender hearts, with it, love and happiness we will dine on. What's left of the surrounding nations will join to praise and worship, and you, Israel, will be their leader. Once again our family will be complete, with all the Saints in their new heavenly bodies, My Holy bride. Even the animals will come to parade and feast with us as friends. On that day, time will stop. This will be the greatest day planet Earth has ever seen. O Israel, we have dreamed of this day for so long, and it is soon to come. Don't hesitate, My chosen people; come and I will give you everything you desire. My love for you will never die. Return home, My people. I will protect you in the night, and in that final hour of testing, your eyes will be opened. That exact moment that you, Israel, wake up and realize who I am, Jesus Christ the Messiah, will be the greatest moment ever recorded.

I, the Lord your God, have spoken!"

The Downfall of Men in Society

The Lord's anger boils at the men of North America.

Listen to the Word of the Lord:

"Where are My men? I have drawn the measuring line. I cannot find My men! Too few remain loyal enough to call My children. You allow your wives to be your mothers too?! You have decayed and gone the way of Ahab. Like him, you have allowed Jezebel to run rampant. You have given her too much power, and she is dictating the important decisions while you sit back and watch. All you care about is making sure she takes care of you like a child with his mother. She is in charge, not you! Stand up and look at how your nation has slipped away. There are not enough good men!

And you women, I will strip all your undergarments off, showing what a prostitute you really are. You want everyone to lust after you? Now they won't have anything to do with you, because your body will be all used up. Like a harlot, people will walk by and scoff at the smell of you. A man cannot walk down the street without lusting and filling his mind with sexual thoughts because of how revealing your dress is. I can tell where a nation is morally by the way its women dress. Like the Greeks, you have shown almost all of your bodies and have lustful imaginations. How many men do you want? These are the things I have against you. And you wonder why I must take action. I cannot count on this nation to lead any longer! If you cannot take care of your own, how can you take care of My affairs?"

Warning Against False Prophets

"Liars! You are so wrapped up in your own selfish prophesies that it makes the Heavens shake! Where have you received your visions and dreams? Not from Me! Why, it has been from the harlot who sits on many waters. She has deceived you and twisted your senses with lies. Much like Jezebel, you have led My people astray. Your hand is out for wealth and splendor to give false testimony and prophesies, which I despise! How can you guide the people, when you don't know the way yourself? You are twisted inside and have bowed down to spirits who have twisted you. I hear you say, 'The world is becoming better and much more peaceful.' Lies! You say, 'Everyone is becoming more caring and righteous.' Liars! You lust after the world. You enjoy the looks and comments as you prophesy prosperity and peace. You soothsayers! You only tell people what they want to hear and spread corruption. You are too self-absorbed in lies and do not even care for My ways!

"In fact, I do not even know many of you. To make matters worse, you dare to use My Word to protect yourselves and others casting unclean spirits away, without My authority. Everything must be done with My consent. I am against you! Instead of leading My people to the Word, you send them packing in twenty different directions of harlotry! I will cause all your visions and prophesies to fail. Good times are not coming! All of your words will backfire in your face. The people will know that you are false when disaster after disaster piles up against your testimony, and you have told them 'all will be well.'

"In the end, the people will stone you, leave you, and chase and abandon you to rot and die alone with your familiar spirits. Even the spirits will eventually leave you once they realize they have no more use for you. And then I will cause you only to see jackals, buzzards, and ostriches, I will send the black goat after you. They will torment you until you realize the very realm you so loved and in which you played the prostitute. Then you will see how much they really loved you by everlasting suffering.

I, the Lord God Almighty, have spoken!"

The Downfall of Unity in Marriage

The Holy Spirit told me to give a message about the failing marriages in our society:

Our Lord has witnessed many of the marriage ceremonies in recent days that do not include Him. This has caused our God to become jealous and angry. Too many times He has seen vows of unity exchanged outside of a Holy church, or without a Holy man to perform the ceremony if done outside the walls of a church. This has greatly aggravated our Lord. Our brother and disciple, Paul, laid the foundation of marriage when he was filled with the Holy Spirit, which can only reveal truth when giving the Lord's instructions. He laid that foundation in 1 Corinthians 7. Too many times our marriages have ended in divorce. God hates divorce, especially for the selfish reason's marriages are ending today. Another problem is the lack of faithfulness to the unity of marriage. You become one when united in marriage, and this lack of respect for one another has grown intolerable.

When the Lord sees that He is not part of this Holy union, He cannot bless it. Without the blessings of our God, a marriage can be doomed. Not basing your marriage on the foundation of Christ will cause the union to be unclean. This gives the evil one more room to creep inside of the marriage and cause separation and sexual immorality. In fact, many marriage ceremonies have become quite a joke. Our Lord sees nothing but comedy, skits, and themes in many weddings nowadays, and He is irritated beyond belief. Do you not know that the ceremony of marriage creates a special bond and is a most precious matter in the eyes of the Lord? Giving yourself to another until death is of great importance and should be done with all the seriousness and love that is required, and our Heavenly Father should be included in this. Too often marriages are ending in divorce, with a rate that is unacceptable in the sight of the Lord. I plead with you who have not done your vows under the Lord to return to Him and renew them for a unity with God. Churches of all kinds will hold a ceremony for you to renew under God. Or simply ask your pastor to perform one in private, with the blessing of our Lord. Not including the blessings of God in your marriage is a frightful thing. Reunite with the love and acceptance of God. He will bless you in more ways than one. Come back to Him; His arms are open.

And now to the abomination of same-sex marriages. Woe to you who are part of this, and woe to the countries that signed this into law and allow these acts to take place. Much like the Greeks and Romans, our country will be judged for this despicable act. We have gone the way of Sodom in sexual immorality and taken a page out of Gomorrah's book when accepting such things. Are we beasts? Are we so indulged in our fleshly desires that all moral concepts have fallen to the wayside? Yes! We have opened the door for Satan to run rampant in our nation. We have flirted with this for far too long, and now God has loosened the walls of protection. Gross immorality through sexual sin and spirits of separation are now driving wedges in our society. Only the Lord Jesus can save us now.

Joshua's Unbelief

The Lord our God told me repeatedly, but I would not listen. I pleaded with Him for over six weeks and presented our case for judgment. I pleaded for hurricanes. I pleaded for earthquakes. I pleaded for another financial collapse. He would not listen or hear my cry. I prayed, cried, and pleaded for any disaster except the one He told me through the Spirit and His Word. I did not want to hear it, and I tried to block out His message from my mind, but He kept calling me and calling me with truth. So I prayed out loud with everything I had, crying out to Him. I prayed continuously for over a month. "What message should I give my people? How will you judge us?" He showed me time and time again, through His Word and the Holy Spirit, and I still would not accept it.

During this month, our enemy, Satan, that dragon, attacked me, more than he ever had attacked me, with everything he was permitted to attack me with. He used every tactic and tormented me for a month, throwing an arsenal of hosts to break me. But I continued to pray the same prayer, even though I knew the answer deep inside, and did not want to believe or give the message. I ignored my faith and refused to accept what our Lord Most High continued to tell me.

Joshua's Vision of Coming Judgment

Then on the morning of November 4th, 2015 the Lord and Father Abraham came to Joshua:

In the Spirit, the Lord took me to the shore of the sea. In front of me, there were many people preparing boats and packing for a long journey. As I stood there, behind me were people all over the beach just watching. Some were standing, some sitting in the sand, all wondering what everyone was preparing for. I could not help but feel convicted for not helping. Then I saw Father Abraham, the father of faith and the father of nations, working diligently and frantically. Abraham kept looking at me as if he were annoyed and disappointed that I was just standing there and watching him, while everyone else was preparing for the voyage. Finally, Abraham became fed up, dropped everything, came over to me very aggravated, and said, "Why aren't you supporting me!? Why aren't you helping!?" Then he walked away and continued his work.

I wondered why he had yelled at me. I then became angry, so I marched over to Father Abraham and shouted, "I do not have a job or instructions, and I have no money to give. So how am I supposed to support you?" All of a sudden, a hand grabbed my arm and forced me back to where I had been standing originally. Like a child I fought the hand as if I were being put in a time-out. I could not shake off the hand. It was like I had no control over it. The hand of God shoved me down and a voice said, "Go to your knees! Now watch the sea!"

I looked as a tugboat came out of the East, heading West in the sea. A cargo freighter followed it. Great lightning was taking place way out to the West, ahead of the tugboat. Behind the cargo freighter came a spectacular warship, filled with tanks and weapons of war. The first tank was huge and pointed directly at the beach. Then I looked back to the East and saw another warship behind that one, heading West. I counted seven warships heading West in all. As I counted, I started crying to God, "No, no, please. No, please!" I looked back to the East, and there were warships and naval ships as far as the eye could see all heading West. There was no stopping this fleet. It was endless in number. Numberless, I tell you! I cried out to God to allow me to compose myself before He took me out of this vision. I knew exactly what this meant. I said to the Lord, "Okay, okay, I'm ready now. I understand." Then the Lord took me back, and I awoke from this vision.

Joshua's Vision Explained

The Lord speaks to Joshua:

"My son, you plead for hurricanes, fires, and floods. Have I not sent them already? Time and time again I caused the winds to send forth disaster, but My people still refuse to come back to Me. You plead for financial disturbances. Have I not shaken the markets of trade enough? I shook one to the ground, and the other caused a great recession. I warned them and gave them plenty of time for repentance. I waited for them to turn back to Me, but still they grow even more violent toward Me.

"And when you plea for earthquakes or tsunamis, your pleas are for your own desires. I cannot accept this any longer. My Saints cry for justice, but they know in their hearts what must take place. How cumbersome and terrible it all must be, but I am with you, always.

"Have I not loosed the protection and shrunk the military? Have I not caused your leaders to become frantic and worrisome? Confusion spreads in the land like leaves in the autumn. I have caused fear to reach the hearts of many with children. America has been ripened. She is almost ready for harvest. Therefore, a great army has been raised up from the East. How awful it will be for the pampered and rich and godless.

"Abraham, I sent because of your faith. For he has been praying for you; now go out and give this message. This is how you must support the commission. I have made a watchman of you. It is sure to happen as I am the Lord your God. Remember, I will be with you always My son. Be strong and courageous. The plumb line is being set. Tell them to tend their lights."

Warning Against Western Europe

The Lord said to Joshua in the night, "Send this message and prophesy against Western Europe."

This is what the Lord says:

"Listen here, leaders and countrymen, I have this against you. You have always laughed and scoffed at the Americans. Who has always been there in your time of need? How many times have you run to them in times of trouble? Countless times they have bankrolled and delivered on your behalf. Countless times they have flexed their mighty muscle for your behalf, whether right or wrong. They have stayed faithful to you, but you have always talked behind their backs and separated yourselves from them every chance you get. When the siege happens, where will you turn? Who will you run to during the collapse? America will no longer be there to protect you. Only I can, the Sovereign Lord Most High, Christ Jesus.

"I have sent frogs among you already, and it will continue. Soon they will invade the Holy places, and they will become deserted. Then, to save your own skin, you will join alliances and make treaties with enemies to keep from being slaughtered yourselves. I told you repeatedly to raise your hands and honor your beloved God of Israel, but you have joined not only the harlot but also the children of pride, that great dragon. Set aside your worldly ways and melt your hearts for Me once again. I have nurtured you for centuries and given you great power and cultures founded in My name—even raising the great Americas that you founded in My name, Christ Jesus. I will never leave you so long as you repent and turn. This I promise.

I, the Lord, have spoken!"

The Eastern Invasion Compared to the Assyrian Takeover of Israel

The constant alarm. The sounding of the horn for days. The whole continent is under high alert. Will the sirens ever cease? Terrifying wails. Fear of black death. Your heart stops. Have you ever seen anything like this? How sudden. What happened? "O Lord, no," they cry. "Why? Why? Why is this happening?!" From out of nowhere! They are relentless! A vast army as big as the sea itself. See the people run like scattering ants on the beaches. Explosions, wrath—the enemy shows no mercy. A great locust army is sweeping the nation bringing fear, treachery, and trembling. The fear causes people to stand still and watch in disbelief. The enemy looks like devils with razor teeth, like lions who have not eaten in weeks. O America, no, no…no! Screams for miles, the sound of terror won't stop! Please let the noise stop; I hear only death! Ahh, stop, stop!

Underground they go as the bombs keep coming for days and days. "No, we weren't ready," the leaders will say, and some will have departed the country as deserters and traders who were given gold and riches for our destruction. Like Assyria, the noise of their warships and soldiers will shake the ground. "Surely, this is the end. O, the prophets of Christ were right," they will say. "Why didn't we listen to the Saints when they repeatedly told us and prophesied to us? The Word of God is real," some will say. But most will scoff, mock and take advantage of the situation.

The Nation of the Cross has fallen! The Nation of the Cross has fallen! Throughout the whole world they will proclaim this. "Who will stop us now?" the mighty nations will say as they gloat in the destruction of America. Parades and festivals will explode in enemy nations when they hear of America's misery. "Now we can take Jerusalem!" they will say. O, how I weep for my country. Please take us, Lord, before this happens, O please, Father. O, Father, please! I beg of you, assemble your people in the clouds, Jesus, before this happens. Let us prepare for the journey, and send us home to be with you, Lord! I cannot stand this vision. It won't leave my memory. O please, Lord God, take your Saints home before this happens!!

The Scattered Remnant

This is what the Lord God of Israel says:

"Blow the trumpet, sound the alarm in Zion! Come now, Israel, take the warning of the Lord your God. Go to

Bethlehem. Go to Jerusalem. Go to Beersheba. Go back to the land of Judah and Benjamin. The throne of David awaits! The New Kingdom is to be set up for only I can protect you there. Nations will be at war soon. Nation upon nation, brother upon brother. You will not survive unless you return, you stubborn people! O, Jacob, will you not listen to My final warning? I have made a place for you, but only the ones who hear My voice will come. Return at once! O, blessed Israel return! I have no more strength to look upon what I have created and have grown weary of this world. This is your final warning. Let My Spirit enter your hearts, you hardheaded fools! I am your Father. Listen! I will send prophets to you, and many will be Gentiles, so do not turn them away! They are My prophets and My servants.

This is the command made to you by the Most High, the God of Abraham, Isaac, and Jacob. The Lord of Hosts has spoken!"

Set Your Differences Aside

"Dear friends, do not believe every spirit, but test the spirits to see if they are from God because many false prophets have gone out into the world. This is how you can recognize the Spirit of God: Every spirit that acknowledges that Jesus Christ has come in the flesh is from God" (1 John 4:1–2).

Love for and belief in Jesus Christ is the one true and most important factor in our Church. Christ did not believe in denominations, and neither should we. Many of our brothers and sisters spend so much time arguing and complaining about the different styles of teaching. There is coming a time when none of that will matter. Baptists will lock arms with Catholics, Methodists will hold hands with Pentecostals, and Coptic's will rejoice with Lutherans. These things should not drive such a wedge in our unity. Heaven will be filled with believers in Christ, as we are all sons and daughters of God. There will be no Lutheran side or Spanish-speaking section of Heaven. We will all be one Church under Christ. Instead of ridiculing each other for our minor differences, we should be in fellowship with one another and working together.

I, too, was once guilty of bad-mouthing the Catholic Church. But when God revealed to me how He used the Catholic faith—to spread the good news to the ends of the earth since the first century—how can we deny it? Then, as fate would have it, God gave me the opportunity to train a man from the Catholic doctrine. His name was Nicholas, and he had just recently decided against his preparation of the Catholic priesthood and was looking for a new beginning. We were able to talk as brothers and discuss the differences between our doctrines. I left our conversations every single time knowing, without a doubt, that he truly loved Jesus Christ. You know what my dear friends? That is good enough for me. I miss talking with my brother, Nicholas. We learned a lot from one another. But what made our friendship strong, was the fact that we were open and willing to combine our knowledge, becoming more flexible in understanding all the different styles of Christianity.

It seems we have become closed-minded and prideful in our faith, instead of saying hallelujah when we hear another person who goes to a church that believes in Christ. We need not bash each other—this world persecutes us enough! You have heard that our Lord despises the doctrine of the Nicolaitans. Therefore, be teachable and open to new beginnings. Do not harden your heart, because our Father cannot penetrate it with truth and different methods to view the scriptures. You see, much like the Pharisees, many scholars and highly regarded theologians are unteachable. As I said earlier, not all are lumped into this group, only those who practice the doctrine of the Nicolaitans. They have formed an opinion and cemented it into the very deepest part of their hearts. So now it is like a precious stone to them, nothing can penetrate it. They hold on to this precious jewel so tight, that no one can take it away from them. They refuse to let anyone hold the jewel. By doing this, nobody can critique the stone and give them advise on what to do with it. The stone must be shaved and cut down, so the true light will be revealed. Instead, the precious jewel is foggy with imperfections all over it. They refuse to listen to godly wisdom, and therefore not even the Angels can break the thicket bush in their hearts and remove the jewel, so it can be fixed.

The last thing we need to do is persecute one another. We must learn to lean on each other and support one another. Times are getting worse. We have been so blessed and spoiled in the West to be able to spread the gospel of Christ, that we have become apathetic and omissive about our faith. Actually, we have become scared to voice our faith in public for fear of unacceptance.

The Great Apostasy is upon us. We need to drop the walls we have put up around our own doctrines and beliefs in the Word of God. We need to get back to the basics in our foundation in Christ, and come together to knock the walls down. We must come together in the name of Jesus. Let's keep it simple and real! If two people love Jesus Christ, they are family! Too many times we make things more difficult than they need to be. The time is coming soon for judgment. We will need each other more than ever when that time comes. Most of all, bring the lost sheep who have strayed away back to Christ and the Church, no matter what denomination they are. Invite them with you, or encourage them to return to their faith at whatever church they may attend. Time is short. The Lord is sending a wake-up call to His Church. So wake up! Look at the big picture. We are losing out there in the world. We are all family. Unite!

"Do not get involved in foolish discussions about spiritual pedigrees or in quarrels and fights about obedience to Jewish laws. These kinds of things are useless and a waste of time. If anyone is causing divisions among you, give a first and second warning. After that, have nothing to do with that person" (Titus 3:9–10).

Warning Against Following Nicodemus

I, Joshua David, received this message from the Lord concerning the Nicolaitans.

This is what the Lord your God says:

"You question everything! Just like Nicodemus who straddled the fence, you do not fully believe in what you have been taught and teach. You are like the religious Pharisees! Your boastful spiritual pride in your theology has gotten the best of you. Are you Job? Have you forgotten that I sent Leviathan to wrestle him in his spiritual pride? Your heads have become fat and because of this you are blinded by your own ego. There is but one book of scriptures! Who are you to question every word I have taught?! Where have you resided other than Earth? Tell me, from Jacobs ladder to My throne, exactly how far is the distance through the 2nd Heaven? Where exactly are the indicated areas from which My Seraphim universally travel to and from Earth? Tell me, you seem to know all things, right Nicolaitans? Exactly what realm do the prideful souls of the departed go? Where exactly have I put the ancient evil souls from the great flood? Where is the Queen of Harlot's realm located? Why do certain inhabitants of the 2nd Heaven pray for you people on planet Earth? Tell Me! You have existed so long. Tell me! Do you not still count the number of years you have lived? I AM Eternity!

"Have you no faith? Do you not believe? What comes forth out of My mouth was, is, and always will be! It is timeless! How are you going to understand heavenly wisdom, if you cannot get past Earth? How frustrating! You are like babies who continue the same discussions over and over and over again. Whining, and forming groups of men who only agree with your own opinions is all that you do. Your tongues are like vipers, pouncing on anyone who doesn't agree with your theory's.

"Joshua, listen to me carefully; They act like hired shepherds who have grown comfortable with their own success. When the wolf comes, they run to the arms of their colleagues, which is their comfort zone. How dare they not sacrifice themselves for the sheep! In their eyes, they have become more important than everyone else. They are blinded by their own ministry but give no thought to the purpose and will of their heavenly Father. Humble yourselves! You have only the authority that I grant, and all I have granted can be taken away swiftly.

"It's no wonder why there is so much division in My Church! It is you! You have caused this to happen! My sheep have been scattered in seven different directions because of your hypocrisy. You spend so much time in debate that you cannot save the lost sheep! Like the Greeks, you form societies and secret clubs who try to push an agenda of your own belief systems. You are supposedly the leaders and chief shepherd's, but Satan has crept into your bedroom and twisted your minds with the spirit of doubt. You look only at rational ideas instead of what the Ancient of Days has spoken! You are the Nicolaitans! You are the Pharisees! Like Nicodemus, you come to Me in the dark of night and question My authority. I have said all that needs to be said, now it is you who must believe in what I, the Son of Man, is saying! Have you been born of the Spirit?

"I am against you for this! This practice produces no fruit in My kingdom and serves no purpose. I send out my disciples to spread the good news, heal this sick, and cast out demons. To be a force of good in this fallen world. Get back to the basics of My teachings and stop the feuding amongst brethren. We are at war and My time is coming soon. I need you to lead your armies, not ridicule and argue over foolish doctrinal issues. Stop putting My Word in a box! Repent of this practice and turn from your ways.

I, Jesus Christ the Mighty, have spoken!"

The Great Apostasy

I was awoken in the middle of the night, and a soft voice said one word to me, *apostasy*, and filled me with the Holy Spirit for sanctification of this message.

We can choose many different reasons for the coming judgment to the West. The Americas are linked to western Europe. Since the fall of Rome, our policies mimic western European policies, so we come from the same loins. The main reason judgment is coming is our apostasy. The falling away from faith in God. We have turned our back on our foundation in Christ. We are living in the age of the "Great Apostasy" written in scripture:

"Don't be fooled by what they say. For that day will not come until there is a great rebellion against God and the man of lawlessness is revealed—the one who brings destruction" (2 Thess. 2:3).

The rebellion has begun, my dear friends. Stay the course and stand firm. This has just begun to take shape. If some of you have walked away from your faith, return at once! God is merciful. He will protect you during the breakdown of our societies. I tell you from my love for you, time is shorter than you think. The Lord has asked me to keep quiet on many visions and sent that leviathan spirit to keep me from getting puffed up with pride when I write to you. But I say unto you, he is coming and has been born into this world already. The false prophet who will make way for the beast is here in human flesh now. Our Lord is moving swiftly across the nations.

Have you not been paying attention? Come now and repent. The Lord will wash your robes clean and take you up to meet Him. He has made a way of escape for His bride, the Church. Get into the Word, and allow the Holy Spirit to teach you. The judgment of Earth draws near. The labor pains have begun as our King Jesus states in Matthew 24. Remember, earthquakes are to follow, along with wars and rumors of war. That statue in New York will be underwater; she is a prostitute. How dare that be put up in our nation, and the people do not even know the meaning behind her. Worldly harlot of Babylon!! The lack of Christ in people's lives has made them fatheads and truly uneducated. We live so worldly that nothing but indulging ourselves in sin seems to be the norm. We salivate in envy and lust; we crave what others have, trying to outdo each other every chance we get. Most of all, children learn from a young age that nothing can fulfill their lust. Always wanting more is the American way. If you have it, I want it too. If I can't have it, I will take it from you. We are like spoiled children. We should be ashamed of ourselves, but no! We feel we are entitled to receive everything. If we don't get it, we cry, pout, and throw temper tantrums like a baby.

No wonder the Lord must step in. He cannot allow this injustice to go on. He must be righteous and true! We are so far from Him that only judgment can set things right. I am sorry for getting upset, dear friends. I just hate to see this unfold before my eyes. And I want to hit home some points that will touch everyone. I, too, have done all those things. I am ashamed about our apostasy. I am ashamed to say this nation was founded on the total principles of God, and look how far we have fallen. That harlot has infiltrated our nation; do you not see? She persecutes the Church into false teachings, false religions, and false ways of living. Like Jezebel, she turns our Church leaders into doing evil! I can't wait to rejoice in Heaven when she, the Mother of Harlots is destroyed from the 1st Heaven! Get back to the Word and know truth! This is just the beginning. Come back! Your very lives depend on it. Eternity awaits us. Where will you go? Think about it. Open your eyes for many of you are blinded.

We All Have a Job to Do

Remember, all Saints have duties that our Father has given us. Do not be discouraged and think that your job is worthless or that it doesn't matter. Every person is an integral part of the Holy system of God. Just as an engine runs, so does the family of Christ. If one single bolt snaps off the engine, it may run for a while, but soon it will cause stress to other parts of the engine. Resulting in the shutdown of the entire engine so that it may be repaired.

Our Church under Christ runs the same way. God gives each person a job or task to do that keeps our system running. The soldiers on the front line cannot fight if they are not fed and given fresh clothes. The injured cannot be loved, nurtured, and cared for without nurses and doctors. The commanders cannot lead if the secretaries do not keep everything organized for them. We cannot receive intercession, help, and guidance from the Lord without the prayer team. There is power in prayer, and prayer warriors are a significant part of the Holy system. We must be a well-oiled machine. Don't get discouraged; God has you exactly where He wants you. Some of you who are comfortable may get moved to a different position, so keep your head up and serve willingly and faithfully. God has a plan for everyone.

God has no favorites. As I said before, you each have a part in the Church, and without you, we cannot run properly. Does the Father love half of His children greatly but the other half only a little? Of course not. The Father loves all His children and cares for each and every one of them, not playing favorites. One may be the lead singer, and the others set up the stage; it is all in the name of Jesus Christ. The Church must run accordingly.

In Heaven, we will have jobs as well. Will you scoff and complain and judge others then? No, you won't because you will serve willingly and with love. So try to keep that attitude here on Earth as well. Lead by the Spirit that is in you. Try to act heavenly because that is what we are striving for. When you do this, others will follow your example. You are leading them to the water. If works are done with joy and love, it will encourage others to join in our family and help the great commission. So remember, our earthly jobs prepare us for the heavenly jobs we will receive.

The Word states that we will receive rewards. Some of those very rewards will be what power and authority each person will receive from Christ in the Kingdom. So I say, strive to get the job you would like in Heaven, by doing what the Father asks of you here on Earth. And don't forget, we will be coming back here with the Lord to set up the Kingdom. It does not take much wisdom to know that we will all be given certain responsibilities as we tend to the remnant Gentiles and tribes of Israel during the 1000-year reign. Christ will have much work to do, and we are His servants. We will be given control of the nations and must teach the remnant well in our heavenly bodies. I love you and may the Lord bless you!

Encouragement in the Puzzle Pieces of God

"Whenever trouble comes your way, let it be an opportunity for joy. For when your faith is tested, your endurance has a chance to grow. So let it grow, for when your endurance is fully developed, you will be strong in character and ready for anything." (James 1:2–4).

To those whom God our Father has given an adventure into wisdom:

Our Lord sometimes will give you a puzzle. But unlike having all the pieces at hand, God will give you one piece at a time. Each piece will make you ponder just what the Lord is trying to teach you. Rejoice in this, my siblings, because you are about to be blessed with wisdom and spiritual knowledge. As we go through journeys in our life, sometimes God will throw a piece of the puzzle to you. At first you will receive just a few pieces and may get discouraged and aggravated, not knowing what they mean or what to do with them. Pray and stay in the Word. Ask the Lord what He is trying to teach you. Be aware of your surroundings, and watch God give you more pieces to the puzzle, but only when you are ready to move on to the next step. Our Lord loves to show off, and during this time, you will see just how many ways He can communicate with you.

As you begin to fit the puzzle pieces together, it will encourage you to depend on God more and more. Your new spirit that Christ gave you will become more in tune with your soul, and He will reveal mysteries and wonders to you in order to help you in life. As each week passes during your new puzzle, if you remain faithful and eager to learn, you will grow excited and anxious about receiving the next piece of the puzzle. Each piece will be like a gem to you as you learn and relate each piece to His Word in your studies. Once you begin to realize how the Holy Spirit counsels you, and that you are receiving direct messages from our heavenly Father, you will realize the power in faithfulness. Be sure to fall to your knees in humbleness to praise and thank the Lord our God, for He is giving you lessons from above, which are priceless.

When you get to the middle of your puzzle, you will be able to look ahead and see what God is trying to teach you, but I assure you that the climax of the puzzle will be more astounding and blessed than you could have imagined. As I said before, our Lord loves to show off. Remember, He will only give you a piece of the puzzle when you are ready for it. He wants to make sure you receive the full benefit of what He is teaching. If you are not ready spiritually and mentally, He will not give it. So be patient, and God will reveal why you are not ready, and then you will thank Him all the more. Be diligent and thankful to God during these times and He will bless you.

"If you need wisdom—if you want to know what God wants you to do—ask Him, and He will gladly tell you. He will not resent you asking. But when you ask Him, be sure that you really expect Him to answer, for a doubtful mind is as unsettled as a wave of the sea that is driven and tossed by the wind." (James 1:5–6).

A Psalm for Christ

O, how you tease me, Lord.

When you touch me, I feel Heaven.

How can I go on when you show me?

Just a taste is too much to bear.

I reach up and beg for you.

What are you waiting for?

You come so unexpectedly.

It is wonderful like your name.

Only you can draw out the darkness inside with your light.

I cannot wait to feel you again, your comfort, your grace.

I do not know whether I am alive on Earth, or with you.

That touch of overwhelming love.

What are you waiting for?

Life is meaningless without you.

It is like a thirst that can never be quenched,

Like a hunger that can never be satisfied.

Paradise is so much better than here.

Take us home so we can be a family!

O Father, your desire is for us to all be together.

O Lord, I can hardly wait to feel your presence.

One second is like an eternity.

What are you waiting for?

You are my everything, my everything!

Pray for Your Shepherds

Dear friends, I come to you today to explain the importance of prayer, which is needed for your leaders of the Church. We all should know the importance of prayer and how vital it is to our everyday lives. But sometimes we expect too much from our elders and chief shepherds. I believe we take them for granted, expecting our leaders to always lend a helping hand and support the sheep. We seem to ask much of them, constantly needing prayer or guidance, which is what a good shepherd should do.

However, have you thought of the pressure and constant attacks from the adversary that the Church leaders must face? They are human and suffer the same challenges as we do, except they endure much more. Satan is always on the attack. One of his best tactics is to attack the shepherds viciously. A shepherd's job is to tend their flock. The enemy knows this; if he can take out the shepherd who feeds and tends to the sheep, many of the sheep will lose their way and become easy targets to devour. It's an old military tactic that is still at work to this day. Distract and preoccupy the master, then the servants will stray and open themselves up to become easy prey.

The Church leaders who spread the good news and keep the will of God flowing to their people are under much more scrutiny and persecution than many believe. The leaders must continue their ministry, no matter what has happened during the week or past month. Many times, they must be centrally active in the Church or ministry, but behind the scenes, those elders are in an all-out war with the enemy, taking all their energy and courage to stand up and lead by example. This can be taxing and take much discipline, my fellow Saints. The more serious you take your faith in Christ, the harder the rules become. This statement is very true. Satan knows who has become a true servant of Christ and a leader among men. Therefore, he has his eye and wicked spirits constantly trying to disrupt the works of the shepherd. So the shepherd must pay close attention to the Spirit of Truth in order to not become confused.

Our elders need prayer and encouragement just like everyone else. Tell them that you love and respect them. Thank them for all they do and let them know that you are praying for them. This will help the elders to know that you are behind them every step of the way. Remember, every person has a job in the body of Christ. Without your support and prayers to everyone in your local church, including the leaders, things could break down. And we don't want to give any ground to our enemy, do we? He has robbed us enough. Let's not let him rob us of our spiritual food that we so desperately need from our shepherds.

Prayer for Our Father in Heaven

Another subject I must touch on, being filled with the Holy Spirit, is the need to pray for our King, Jesus Christ. Do you realize that even He needs prayer? If we are the bride of Christ, should we not pray for our groom? Does a wife not pray for her husband? Of course she does. Therefore, I say we must pray for Jesus, our Savior. I come to you as a messenger of God when I say that what will take place in the near future is going to be the most difficult and heartbreaking task our Lord must do—that is, deciding when He will take His bride, which is the Church, up, removing them from this world, and forgo tribulation and judgment of the Earth and nations. Remember, we are not of this world, therefore, we will not be judged according to this world. We are citizens of Heaven and children of God once we have received the Holy Spirit, no longer being citizens of Earth. This event is not something that will be joyful or pleasing in any way. Yes, we will meet as one in our heavenly bodies with Christ. But the destruction and death that will come directly afterward, down here on this planet, will be filled with sorrow and treachery. When the seals, trumpets, and bowls are unveiled, it will be hell on Earth. As it is written, nothing like it has ever been seen on the Earth.

Scripture says only the Father knows the day and hour when these events will take place. Not even the Angels know the exact time this will take place. So I say, pray for our Father. Pray that He has the courage, strength, and will to do what is necessary to this world. Pray that He gives the order to swing the ax of justice to the nations. Pray that Christ has the strength and will to fulfill what must be done. This will not be a glorious time in Heaven. Many people will die, and sin will fill the Earth during these days, as the man of lawlessness sits among the nations. We are the body of Christ, and so our heart is His heart, which means we love as He loves. Heaven is filled with love, and the Father does not wish to see such death and sorrow that must take place soon. We will all be in mourning when these events take place. So pray for our Father because He will need our love with Him during this time of decision. What terribleness it will be. Who will enjoy the destruction that must take place to cleanse the Earth? No Holy being or creature will. It will be done with a heavy heart, head, and hand. Pray for the One who is Holy and wears the crown. He will need all the love and support He can get from His Saints.

2 Joshua David

The Lord Relents His Judgment

It was autumn, in the year of our Lord 2016, during President Barrack Obama's final year of reign. The Lord Jesus Christ was set to judge North America. I, Joshua David, a seer for Christ, along with other prophets across the country, had been preparing for disaster. We set out preaching that judgment was coming soon. To repent and turn to the Lord, so He may show mercy and protect His Saints during the harsh judgment that was to come. This was a time when no kings or monarchs ruled the land. A voting system was in place to give power back to the people. The citizens of our nation would hold a vote, and whoever won that vote would be named: The President of the United States of America. Every four years this vote took place so one man could not rule for too long. Eight years was the maximum time that one man could reign as president. America was coming to a boil. The Lord God Almighty gave multiple messages to me in October 2016 and commanded me to document them.

This is what the Lord says:

"I have witnessed the abominable acts taking place in your country. I have grown increasingly tired of the people in this land and of My Saints who refuse to unite and speak up. I issue this decree: If you do not come back to Me and take hold of your country, Saints, I will forgo judgment. You are hanging on by a thread that has been splintered and torn.

This warning is for you: If that wretched woman Hillary Clinton is voted in as the next ruler of your land, I will pour out My wrath from Heaven and strike you down for all the nations to see. I will cause famine and disease like you never have seen in the history of your country. I, the Lord God Almighty, will give you one last chance to fast and pray for your land in these final weeks leading up to the vote. You want to see if I am merciful? Challenge Me! Go ahead and challenge Me! See what I will do for My children if they will just unite and do what is right in their spirits. If they do not, I will move swiftly and cause destruction in the land as never seen before in its history.

I, the Lord your God, have spoken."

And so it was. Over the final four weeks leading up to the vote, the Spirit of the Lord moved on all Saints of the land with heavy conviction. Prophets, priests, and shepherds alike had one message to the Church: Repent and turn to the Lord your God. Unite and stand on the principles of the Word of God. The Christian vote is the Republican vote. Follow the guidance of the Holy Spirit, and maybe our God will show mercy to us all. This was preached over the entire nation and on all airwaves. I witnessed this great movement with my own eyes, as this was a time of great technology in the world. Grace was made available for the Americans to take by faith.

The Saints Respond

This is what the Lord says:

"O My children, I knew you would come back to Me. I have heard the cries of My Saints. Although there are so few, I see that you still love Me and hold Me close during these final days. All of Heaven is rejoicing. You have seen what has been taking place in your land and have stood your ground for Me. Therefore, I will relent for your sake, Saints. Because I love you so dearly, I will not send judgment to your nation at this time. I will not forgo the end; I will hold off just a little longer. Because you have turned to Me, I will not judge your lands during the reign of Donald Trump. During his reign, I will build up your protection and bless you. O, Holy Saints, how you bring Me joy. Rejoice! Call a festival! Have fellowship! You have made Heaven proud, and I will never forget what you have done My dear children. You have been victorious! My gift to you is time; spend it wisely with Me and your families.

"This one command I leave you: America, strengthen the Church! I said strengthen the Church! You have extended your time just a short while, so unite the Church. Your nation's sins have roots that go deep. They have taken root so deep that soon

I will have no choice but to uproot them. Teach your children My ways; be vigilant for My sake. I command you to be vigilant in spreading the good news. I will be with you always. Take courage, for I will never forsake you.

I, the Lord God Almighty, have spoken."

A Song of Praise and Repentance

I shall humble myself in front of the great and mighty Lord.

I will take refuge in my God, knowing that I am filled with fleshly pride.

Only He can reveal what is in my heart, which is wrapped with vines and thorns.

Our great Christ can untwist them and break the root of the thicket bush in my heart.

He shows me through His Spirit what I am.

He shows me through His Spirit what I must become.

I am willing to change, my great God.

You have revealed my inner selfishness.

You have shown your great and awesome love by doing this.

I see now, O how wrong I was and didn't realize it!

Great Mighty One, I cry out to you with a thankful heart now!

O how pride blinds; I can see again because of you, Jesus.

And I will recommit myself to your ways once again.

The Lord Curses the Nations

On December 23, 2016, during the final month of President Obama's reign, the United Nations held a World International Vote in East Jerusalem on land where the Temple Mount is located. That land, which is Holy to Christians and Jews, has been disputed by the Muslim Palestinians of Hamas for centuries. These people are descendants of the ancient Philistines. The vote was passed unanimously by a 14–0 margin, giving the rights to build and occupy the land over to Palestinian and Muslim control. This is the same Holy land that the prophet Daniel spoke about when he said an image of desolation will be put up during the great tribulation. Earth had begun its labor pains at the turn of the millennium, and now the Lord had begun to rapidly fulfill all of His promises through the prophets. Directly after this vote, over the course of three months, I received multiple messages from the Lord about the fourteen nations around the world that voted against Israel.

Here is the list of Nations that held power over Jerusalem's fate and voted against the Judean Covenant.

- China
- United Kingdom/Great Britain
- Venezuela
- Malaysia
- Japan
- Angola
- Ukraine
- France
- Russia
- New Zealand
- Egypt
- Senegal
- Spain
- Uruguay

Egypt's Devastation

This is what the Lord El Shaddai says:

"Nation of lies and deceit. Nation that's filled with every perversion imaginable. How My anger has reached its zenith with you! You little twisted snake. I will chop your head completely off in the last days, which are soon to come. This generation! How dare you cozy up to My Jacob, and then just like Delilah you run to mischief. Abdel Fattah el-Sisi, ruler of Egypt, your name from now on will be Delilah. Orchestrating the draft of this world law was your final demise. I will throw Egypt into the Valley of Hinnom with all your soldiers. Your nation will beg for mercy, but I will not hear their cries. In the valley, a man gets to know himself. In the valley, death surrounds him. Alexandria, wail! Cairo, scream! For terror is coming like you have never seen; even the ancient cities will cry out with the magnitude of your destruction. The hook will draw you into the Valley of Slaughter, along with the immoral nations with whom you have fornicated. Just when you had your strongest ties with Jacob in decades, you cut his hair. That's my land! My temple! You still call yourself an ally? Lies! Now other nations will use you like a worn-out prostitute. You want it? You got it! You have come against Me again as in days past, but you forget My wrath. You should know Me better than anyone! I set My anger upon you, Egypt.

I, Jesus Christ the Mighty, have spoken!"

A Message to France

The Lord then said to Joshua, "Turn thy face over to France and give them this message."

Hear the Word of the Lord:

"France, with all your vanity and sexuality, the world lusts for your prim and proper ways. The city of love is ruled by the Great Harlot. I will throw you down along with her and ancient Babylon. You are a product of Babylon! Immoral city who runs to infest itself with her cup of death. Nothing but crows, buzzards, and every foul bird reign on her lands. The jackal and wolf Nephilim are her lieutenants. The Behemoths serve as her generals and bow down to her, because they couldn't control their flesh during the ancient world. She makes her headquarters in the atmospheric realm and looks down from the moon. Nice statue of her you have there. Abomination! It seems like I've noticed her idol before with your other adulteress, North America. Both of you are sisters. Don't think I didn't see your schemes against My Israel. How dare you leave Me after all I have given you. What happened to your love for Me? You love everyone else, but what about Me? My heart is bleeding by your stab on that vote.

"I've warned you repeatedly for the past decade. 'Turn back to me!' I shout, but you do not listen. 'Humble yourselves!' I scream, but your ears are deaf. Your infatuation with yourselves and love for others has gotten the best of you. These are the facts that have been presented to Me in the Courts of Heaven. I must be just. Luke warm followers of the Way. You better come back to Me, and I mean quick. I am running to you, My children; can't you see Me? Do you still know the voice of your Father? Have you forgotten Me? I have not forsaken you. Turn and come back. I miss you! Let Me heal you!"

A Message to the United Kingdom

Then the Lord spoke again. "Send this message to Britannia."

This is what the Lord says:

"I have issued a special curse to each and every nation that has voted for this. Fourteen of you in all, and you know exactly who you are! United Kingdom? Not so united, are you? Despicable how you have turned your back on me. There is a great crisis in your lands. What is this crisis, you ask? My churches have come up missing! I am sending missionaries to your lands. Can you imagine? I, the Lord God Almighty, am sending missionaries to Britain, Ireland, and Scotland. Not long ago, you were My greatest kingdom to spread the gospel. Now I am forced to send the Word to you from distant lands. What has become of you? Look how far you have fallen! Wake up! I still love you! I am trying to shake you, but you're sleeping or in some sort of trance. Are you drunk? Wake up! Wake up! My children, wake up! Your leaders just went against My Jacob. Do you not even care?"

Future Destruction for Russia

Hear this from the King of Kings who judges the nations:

"To the sides of the North, Russia, and you particular sons of Japheth, you say to yourselves:

'Nobody can push us around. We are high and mighty. There is no God who can stop us. Our strength is in our might and will. Man is superior on the sides of the North; no one is as mighty as we.' You puff your chest and say, 'We are conquerors. We are hunters. We are like the ancient men of renown, powerful on all sides.'

"I, Elohim, the Chief of Heaven's Army, have smelled the stench of your pride unto the 3rd Heaven, even unto the very inner sanctuary of My throne. I have plans for you. This is a warning. I will not bleed you soon. But what your pride gains, I will make you suffer tenfold. My vengeance is upon you. I Myself will come down to judge some of your sons and grandsons, Japheth. I must backhand these arrogant children of yours. For they have defied the living God! Gomer, your time is long overdue, holocaust murderers! Meshech and Tiras, a twinkling in the eye will bring all your armies down to My nation of Israel. Look how beautiful she is. Her breast full and enticing; how will you be able to resist her? 'Come Tubal,' she calls. She cries out, 'Magog and Togarmah, I'm lying in wait for you. Come.' Then as your lust becomes overwhelming, you will come across Hinnom; all your soldiers will see into My eyes there. You will say, 'Who is this Son of the Most High? Have we been tricked? Terror is like none other in my heart.' You will melt. Fear will overcome you on that day. Death is near to you.

"Young soldiers are ignorant of what they are about to endure when they become men. A funnel will appear, and there is nothing you can do to stop it. I will cause pride and lust to entice all descendants of Japheth whom I have mentioned into my pit. There are no men to stand in the gap for you. Too few are in your lands. However, I will send mighty Angels, even Gabriel, to save My children on your lands before I draw your nation into the slaughter. I will have My vengeance. It is all mine.

I, Jesus Christ the Mighty, have spoken!"

To The Nation of the Cross

This message is from a Father's broken heart:

"I look to you, My darling America, but you refuse to look back at Me. I beg of you as a father on His knees to come back. But when I consider your eyes, they are cold. Something has happened to your eyes. They…they are blank. It's as if there is no color in them anymore. Your eyes have glazed over, and when I look into them, I cannot find My daughter. Where is she? Where is My little girl? Has she left Me? My worst nightmare has happened! My daughter…My daughter has left Me. I didn't want to believe it, even when the report came back from My Holy Seraphim. They had to call out My name seven times because I couldn't look them in the face. They told Me what you did. The ones who protect you came up to My throne with tears in their eyes as they prepared to give Me the report. I cried out, 'No! No! Don't tell Me what they said. Don't tell Me what they did. My heart is already torn; don't break it!'

"But as My Seraphim soldiers came into My presence, they dropped their shields because they were heavy with grief. They took off their helmets and placed them before Me. They drove their swords into the ground and fell to one knee. With tears in their eyes, they said:

'The Nation of the Cross could have stopped this vote, but instead they didn't vote at all. They allowed this to take place. One vote against could have stopped it, but they...they, um, Dad...they...'

And I couldn't hear it come out of their mouths. So I asked them to leave My presence for a moment. As We wept, Heaven became silent. And then I knew My heart was broken. I knew that I couldn't wait any longer. I reluctantly had to go forth with the end of the age. Why, America? I loved you. I love you still. You were special to Me, but things are different between us now. Come back My lost ones. Come back to the arms of your Father. Please?"

Warning for a Beloved

"O Tarshish, listen to your Father for a moment. Go to a place and shut the door. Bow your head, but don't speak; just listen to Me. I am the one whose voice is soft to His children. I discipline with authority, and My voice is the sound of many waters, as My will must be done. But when My children have lost their way and forgotten their first love, My voice is soft. I call out to you. Do you hear Me? Can you hear Me? I know many of you. You are suffering. Don't let Jezebel speak lies into your hearts. She has been slowly whispering abominations into your ears for centuries. Remember your light stand; I am your first love. I am the beginning, the end, and all that will come. My promise still stands. You still have a choice to be rescued from the time of great testing and tribulation, but that window is closing fast.

"Tarshish, your descendants have conquered distant lands with great power. I gave you this power. Who has set your bow portside? Who gave you the eastern winds? Who set your sail west, across the great sea to the New World? For it was Me. Your light shined for all to see in the days of your travels, but now that your great conquest is over, your light is flickering. On some nights, you cease to even turn on your lighthouse. Shouldn't your lighthouse go on every night? You have become passionless, and as a result, Jezebel has overtaken your places of worship — and that, I cannot stand for. Babylon is not the way, I am. Something great and terrible is coming, and I will draw you into this conflict. Set your ships to sail for Me once again, and I promise you relief in the days ahead. But if you refuse, and continue to be deceived by that witch, I cannot protect you.

"I will give you this last gift now because I love you so much, so listen to the words of your Father:

"Because so many of you will go through the tribulation, don't give up hope! Stay encouraged! I still love you. I will never leave you. You stay with Me and set your light ablaze, so no man can blow it out. I will use you in ways that have never before been seen on this planet during this time. Be courageous! Don't get discouraged! I will send forth My Spirit in many ways, so you will do great miracles and signs. This is My will so that many still have a chance to repent and see that I, Jesus Christ, am merciful and give an opportunity for each name to remain in the great book. I will have armies of Angels with you, so stand up for what is right and win many souls during this time. My glory is with you who are left, so be good servants. You will be with Me once again, so be patient and win many for My sake.

These are the commands of Jesus Christ the Mighty!"

Complete Annihilation of the Philistines

The Lord said to His servant, "Look to the Philistines and prophesy against them. Write down every detail of the words I speak to you, for they are very important."

This is what the Chief Commander of Heaven's Army says:

"Since I brought Jacob across the Jordan, I have had to put up with your abominations. You simply *will not* go away. I have made you a thorn in the side of My children, but soon that thorn will be plucked out and thrown into outer darkness. Ashdod, Gaza, Gath, and all Palestinians will be assembled. I will bring you to Bozrah. The river Jordan will be your final taste. Your horses will drink one last time there. Look around, take it all in, because you will never see your home land again. When you arrive in Bozrah, the vast armies of the nations will startle you. You will look with amazement and say to yourselves, 'What does our small army have to offer this massive military campaign? All this just to defeat Jacob?' When you stand on that ground and get into formation, you will know your fate. I will send locusts from the pit to fill you with fear.

"On that day, the heat of the sun will be unbearable, and many soldiers will collapse as they stand in their lines. Then, coming in the clouds, I, the Son of Man, will set My foot down in Bozrah with fury, crushing the serpent's head. On that day, I will set My anger upon you. I will burn in the fire all the inhabitants of the serpent's tail up to Hinnom. There, a great victory will be proclaimed. I, the Son of Man, will be seen on Zion, lifted up with glory for all to see. A great shout like thunder will go across the Earth, and My children will know it is the voice of their Father. Streets will be filled with tears of joy. Jacob will rejoice and bow facedown to the Lord their God. The Gentiles will proclaim victory in the name of Jesus Christ! Chants of My name will ring across Earth, even the Earth itself will rejoice with grumblings and put forth new life."

This song will be proclaimed throughout the world as all tongues and kindreds march to the great celebration feast in Jerusalem to honor Christ:

We glorify your name, Lord.

Forever and ever your name is glorified.

From Zion, He shouts, "Victory!

A great victory has been won!"

I will follow the Lord my God!

For He is worthy.

And only He is worthy!

Victory for the children of God!

Victory for the Angels of God!

Victory to our Great King!

Victory!

A Message for Luanda

The Lord spoke from His Holy mountain and asked, "Who is this city of Luanda? What shall I do with such despicable and disgraceful leadership?"

I said to my Lord, "You know best, for I am just your servant."

The Lord responded, "Yes, but what would you do with such abominations?"

I replied to the Holy One, "Please be merciful to Luanda, for they are very poor. The strong oppress the poor and line their pockets with riches. The weak stand no chance against such tyranny. They are but slaves to the filthy rich. And only a very select few hold the keys to the city. They make blood diamonds out of men. They sell men for a day's wage in the mines and go into women as they please. The lavish lifestyle of the wealthy refuse to even give clean drinking water to the poor. Yet they live in the high-rises, gorging themselves with every lust imaginable. The scales at their markets are tipped to trample the weak. The seaports are among the best in the world, but men who work in them feel soulless. O Lord, please have mercy on the poor. I know you are a loving God filled with grace. I know your love is greater than all the Heavens."

The Lord responds, "Very well, I will strike down their markets and bust the legs of the oppressors. No longer will they have slave traders and diamonds with the stain of a thousand men on them. The rich will beg the weak in due time. They will be brought down to the depths of which they despise. An uprising is in store for the oppressed, and I will hand them victory. But this land will never be the same, and I shall hear few cries for My name in her final days.

I, Jesus Christ the Mighty, have spoken."

Destruction for Dakar

Listen, the Lord of Heaven's Army speaks:

"Certainly, you have not heard My warnings time and time again. You Lebanese who live in this foreign land should know My vengeance upon those who try to destroy Jacob.

Your banking industry will go into default, and you will beg for mercy. Other nations will do nothing but scoff at you. You will be weak and helpless. Like a beggar at the markets, people will step over you and spit in disgust. I despise the slave traders. At one time you had many Saints on your lands, but now all forms of life have decayed from pride. Mosques have invaded your nation. Soon enough, the time of the end will come upon you. I pray that a great light will shine from the West, so your eyes will be opened. Look, I come quickly. Seek where you came from as a child, Dakar. Only then will you hear My voice."

To the Inhabitants of Japan

Then the Lord said, "Joshua, send this message to Tokyo."

This is what the Lord says:

"Relentless judgment has come your way for a century. Yet you still do not learn and turn from your ways. I have given you plenty of opportunity to repent, but your pride has fueled a fire in your burning heart. However, your heart doesn't burn for Me. What say you? Have I not decimated your lands time and time again? Every time you take a step forward, you fall back two steps. Consider your ways! It is Me who is holding you back. You refuse to acknowledge My existence, and many of you play the harlot with all your false gods. Sexual perversion of the highest degree fills the dark places in your city.

"I have been merciful and have caused the disasters to hit all around you, but this next one will hit home. You're too close to My sword of judgment, and no allies will save you. What is left of your military will join this nation by force, not by your own accord. I used the Americans as My Holy instrument to backhand you in the past. Yet now that you've become friends, you still refuse to listen to My ways. There is an army coming that no man can count. There is nothing that can stop it. Never before in the history of Earth has there ever been an army so vast, for it has been set up to perform My will on the nations."

A Message to Singapore and Kuala Lumpur

"You build your cities on high and say, 'We are unstoppable.' As a member of the free world, you show how little you know, as well as your age. You've grown too quickly, and now you have taken all the credit. Your heads have become fat. I will break you into submission with one blow. You have no stamina and will fall as fast as you have risen. I will drive you out of your harbors and into the hands of a nation so fierce that you will crumble with fear. Without warning they will overcome you. Like locusts they will strip the land in one large sweep. In a single night, your entire nation will be lost and in the hands of the Chinese. They will move in and set up their camps as if they have lived in your lands for centuries. Depression will devastate you, as you are powerless to the new regime. Those who call on the name of the Lord will have victory over their circumstances. I will give them peace. They will be My children forever and will be victorious over the second death.

I, Jesus Christ the Mighty, have spoken."

The Lord's Tool of Judgment

On March 8, 2017, during the first year of Donald Trump's reign, I, Joshua, received this message from our Lord Jesus.

"I have heard your prayers, My son. I know your fears. I know that you're hesitant to believe what the Spirit is saying. The Spirit that I have given you speaks only truth. This is My voice; it calms you and speaks softly. The waters are still when I speak to My children. For I love you and will be with you always. Listen to what the Spirit says and write these things:

"I have raised up a nation that strikes fear into the heart of all other nations. When people hear of this vast army, their knees tremble and grow weak. Many refuse to speak of the Chinese because they know in their hearts that treachery comes with them. No army ever assembled has been so strong; it is numberless. Right now, they are extending their borders by creating military bases in the open seas. They will smite and plunder the nations around them, and nothing will stop them. The sickle is in their hands to harvest the crop, and this world has been ripened. I will use the Chinese much like the Assyrians and King Nebuchadnezzar of Babylon. As they march to a land, they will conquer it fully and add to their numbers and weaponry. They will be My chastening rod of choice. The descendants of Joktan will no longer be forgotten. For I have made them mighty in the last days.

"Then I will turn them to the West. They will look upon a weak and stumbling North America. Their eyes will lust at the power they can gain by thrusting North America off world-power status. The coastal cities will be decimated. I will completely destroy California for their haughty insolence. Sin City will be no more. The Northeast will see every detestable idol smashed into pieces, and bodies will float on the shores washing up for months. Famine and disease will strike the nation like never before. Flee for the hills; flee to the northern Canadian air. Leave everything at once, and run for your lives; the hand of the Mighty One is upon you. Even as we speak, with all your pride, you are reluctant to talk about the power and overwhelming might of China. Already, China has taken the psychological advantage of your will and fight. Your face cannot hide fear. Run to the South while you still can and repent.

"My name still stands firm in the heart of your country. I will cause the resistance in the Southern States and the heartland just west of the Mississippi to harken unto My voice and grow strong. That is where My belt is fastened. I hear My children's voices there; they cry out to Me, and I will send them aid. I will not completely destroy the heartland. Listen to the words of the solemn Lord your God. I know that you have stayed true to Me ever since I created your nation. You have taught your children well during these terrible times, and for that I am proud of you. Therefore, I will raise up prophets in the

South to guide you into battle just like in the days I was with Judah. Listen and obey them, for they are My servants. They will keep you from harm's way and protect you until the rapture. Remember My promises. Meditate on the scriptures.

"Now, I want to ask you a question. Do you love Me? Do you trust Me? Will you still call out My name? Will you call upon the Lord your God with all your heart and all your soul? Will you glorify My name in these last days? Then stand with Me one last time, My children. Rise up in the face of tyranny and shout My name! Never forsake Me! I will never forsake you! You are My heart and My belt! Rise up! Rise up, children! Now is the time! Give Me everything you've got! Victory is just around the corner. Stay true till the very end, and I will reward you with My Kingdom. I do not leave My children stranded; just like Judah, I promise to always protect you. Don't follow the immorality of the Northeast and West Coast. I am with you! Hold fast Church! Hold fast! I'm coming!

I, Jesus Christ your savior, am coming!"

The Sleeping Bear

Beware the wrath of the bear. Bears pay no attention to others because fear is not found in them. They care only for themselves. No predator dares go up against the bear, for if it does, only death comes its way. They are perfectly at peace and content to be left alone to do their daily routines. The sleeping bear is to be left alone, not to be awakened. But you, America, have awakened the bear! And now the beast has set its eyes on you. The beast looks and salivates at the taste of your flesh.

The Lord sharpens His sword and polishes it for execution. Who can stand in His way? Your shipping industry will cease. Your imports, cut in half and cost twice the amount. China's intel will subdue your forces, they will be like a serpent in the midst of your private matters. The Pentagon will have a snake's nest in it. Vipers will pounce at just the right time. America's leaders have put their trust in those who will betray them. Your technology will fail because the one who holds the key is in the hands of the enemy. Blackouts and power will be lost throughout North America. The enemy is near! They have slowly planned this for decades! Like a strategic mastermind, they will overcome all of your futile military campaigns. Thinking of every possible situation, China will have every maneuver and counteraction that you retaliate with covered to perfection. Every single attempt to counterpunch will only result in frustration and loss of heart. America's pride will be shattered, and for the first time, our nation will beg. On your knees! The world will hear the sobbing of a desperate nation, but none will harken unto our misery.

North America's Leaders

"Hired assassins, racketeers, extortionists, and adulterers fill your lands. The leaders only look out for their bottom lines, as Mammon has darkened their hearts. Conspiracies and political propaganda have filled every household only to promote their agenda. Lies and fabricated stories are told to twist the population into submission. I will break you! You have come against My Holy and righteous children, and for that My anger is boiling. You manipulate everyone around you to get what you want and then dispose of the ones who don't follow along with your plan. How far have you fallen, America? To the depths of Hades?

"On My Holy mountain, I created you as the most precious cherubim, more beautiful than the onyx and jasper. But indignation was found in your heart. For the first time, the sides of the North entered in sin. You took My love and trampled it with your feet, persuading many of My sons with your filth to join you. I cast you down. No longer were you able to dwell in the presence of the Most High and corrupt My Holy ones in the 3rd Heaven. As a result, you made the 2nd Heaven your domain as sin entered all that dwell within it. You corrupt all that is seen, but you will not corrupt that which is unseen! I will keep My Holy mountain precious only to My children, who love Me with all their heart and all their soul. Then, you looked upon Earth and lusted after her too, corrupting My special creation. So very soon you will be cast down even farther and chained upon that rock. I will torment you there, where Hades and Tartarus are prepared for you and your hordes.

I, Jesus Christ the Mighty, have spoken!"

Coming Judgment for China

The Lord of Heaven's Army spoke again, saying, "Write this letter to the descendants of Joktan. Let them know that My sword is upon them, for Holy is My name."

This is what the Lord says:

"Your conquest will be short-lived, Joktan. I have given you power for a short while, but soon enough you will fall. I have made your grave the valley of Jehoshaphat. Great is your kingdom, but all the plunder you receive will not be enjoyed. Your heart is filled with darkness, as the dragon is with you. All your riches will soon be forgotten when the sound of the great trumpet permeates throughout the world, and all are redeemed who have kept My name. I will cause confusion among your elite, and they will send your armies in different directions. For the false prophet will speak lies unto you. But in the end, I will assemble you where you belong. For the day of the Lord's wrath is upon you!"

A Proclamation of War

In the winter of 2017, the Lord sent this message to Joshua:

"Son of man, you are nearing the graduation of your priesthood. You have eaten the words of the Holy prophets and all that is written in the scriptures. You have served in My house humbly and have studied under the elders who have taught you well. The Spirit I have given you has taught you truth and wisdom. I, the Lord Jesus, have now made you ready for service in My great army.

"Now, I have heard the scoffers and the faithless who call you crazy and make you the target of their jokes. I have seen your fellow brethren, even some elders, look with unbelief as you prophesy judgment. Some laugh and pay no attention, but others look upon you with the jealousy of Saul. I will show them that I mean business. Pack your belongings and enter the Academy. I need you to grow accustomed to the art of war. Let everyone know that what you are doing is in the name of the Lord. It is time for you to get militarized. I will make your name great and make you a leader among men. All will listen to your words with great respect, as everything you do will be for My kingdom. As My servant Samuel led the armies of Israel, so you, Joshua, will lead the armies of America."

So I did what I was instructed to do. I entered the Academy. My heart and soul were dedicated to protect and serve my country. And the Lord our God was with me. Then this message came to Joshua from Jesus while in the Academy:

"Your actions will be a demonstration of what is to come. War will be upon the people in your country until the day I return; many will starve and be driven from their homes. Only a select few will make it to the South, where I will protect them. Others will be held captive and shipped to distant lands, forced to join a military not of their own. Some will be held in camps, much like prisons, only to die of disease and famine. The large cities will be decimated; to look upon them will bring great shock and despair. Then, finally, I will have broken the will and pride of so many lost children in your lands. They will repent and call out to Me, and I will come to them."

The Antichrist Rises

Feel the heaviness of smoke rising out of the pit, for Abaddon awakes, the son of perdition. Eyes will look in terror, for he is fear. Great earthquakes devour the land, then suddenly the volcanic eruption that has chained down the lawless one will burst forth out of the smoke and heat of the explosion. The Earth cries out as she cannot contain Abaddon any longer. She spews him out of the fiery depths of the abyss. And the smoke of his torment fills the Earth. Who will be able to stand? Who will be able to survive without calling on the name of the Lord? Abaddon's smoke will be seen by many as it forms. They will look in awe but not understand, for this is just the beginning. The lawless one will do his work secretly and prepare for his time. The Lord God, King of Kings, will smite Abaddon in His fury! The Lord's voice thunders, "Blasphemous Creation!" as the hosts of Heaven are shaken. Never before has the Commander of Heaven's Army been so violent with rage, for the King of Kings has become mad and uncontrollable! His temper vengeful. Lightings and fire burst forth from within His lions as wrath fills His tongue.

The Lord turned to me and shouted with thundering's:

"Have you seen Mecca and the fornication of abominations?! Do you see the people as they twist in the form of the pit like locusts, spiraling down the funnel into the blackness of the hole? I will utterly destroy you, Mecca, and your unholy Kaaba stone by the fire that spews from my wrath! I am the Lord God Almighty!

"Here this, Abaddon, son of Satan, you beast! As soon as your umbilical cord is cut from your mother, the Great Harlot of Babylon, you will be no more. Your name will be erased and forgotten. For My Son, Jesus, is the only name! He is the Holy One! He has all authority! My son, Jesus, is the Great Conqueror! For His name will be exalted above all things! He is Truth! For He is!"

A Generation Rejected

The Lord speaks:

"Look, Joshua, at these so-called millennials. See how they twist even the most just and righteous into heaps of rubble. With their lies and misguided thoughts, they will stop at nothing to get what they want. A spoiled, pampered bunch they are. They have earned nothing; everything has been gift-wrapped and handed to them. Parents rarely discipline, and now they expect everything for nothing. They have grown intolerant of the ways that have made your country great. They spit in the eyes of anyone who disagrees with their opinions. This generation does not know the Lord their God, and therefore, I have rejected this generation. They grow violent toward morality and what is written in the Word. Their outright defiance to all authority is sickening. They refuse to listen to truth because it will spoil their motives. They reject the power that could make their nation godly because of stubbornness and arrogance. They form groups and line the city streets in protest to get what they want. Everything has become offensive to them, but they continue lying, deceiving, and conforming rules to fit their own schemes. Hypocrites! They conspire like crows who gossip together deciding who to defame and destroy. What are they so upset about? Why have they rejected me? Have I not made America the greatest nation ever to be formed on Earth?

"So hear this from the Lord of Heaven's Army: I will strike down this nation and cripple the Northeast. Philadelphia, Washington, and Boston will scream in terror. New York, Detroit, and Chicago will wail at the burning of their cities. The putrefaction of the Golden Coast up through Seattle will be smelled throughout the world. Your metro areas in the West will become wastelands. Uninhabitable! How will your technology save you when all systems have crashed? The millennials will be frantic because they can do nothing with their hands, for they are fat, lazy, and rely on everyone else to make life easy for them. Can they work a day's hard labor without whining and complaining like an infant? No! They will wither away and die off. They will put up no fight as they are exiled off like cattle, going from one place to another begging for food and drink.

"But as for My people who obey My Word, they will be well prepared. For I have sent messengers from Heaven to speak to My priests and prophets. My Spirit will open their eyes with wisdom, as they know the history of My judgments.

I, Jesus Christ the Mighty, have spoken!"

Setting a New Foundation

Listen to the message from the Chief Commander of Heaven's Army:

"Is a home built with no footing? Is a palace built before you hit bedrock? Do you set brick without anchoring in the dowels?

"Then tell Me, how am I supposed to save this great nation without excavating the land first? I must lay out a blueprint. Therefore, I sent My angels to survey the land and file a report to Me on the information they gathered. And let Me tell you, the report wasn't very good. Nevertheless, this is what the Lord God of Israel says: I love this nation as I love Israel. Joy fills My Spirit when I look upon you. You, America, are the leader of the Western world, and I intend to keep it that way heading into the millennial reign when I make My return.

"Listen to the words of the Lord of Heaven's Army: I will appoint a king for you; a new covenant will be set. He will reign from the mountains and hills of the Southern Appalachians. And his family's descendants will sit on the throne forever. Timothy, my sweet Timothy, will reign as I make My return. He will honor Me with a full heart, and I will be with him. His descendants will prosper, and I will always speak through them.

"But first I will cleanse this land, purging it so that it will produce the correct fruit. I must strip the Americans naked until they hit rock. You will dig and dig until you think that you cannot dig anymore. You will cry out to Me! 'Lord! Lord please! We have learned our lesson! Jesus, our King, have mercy upon us!' You will shout, 'Grace! Grace! Grace! Grace!' Tears will roll down your face as you shout My name, begging hysterically for blessings once again. Utterings unheard of, except for in Heaven, will come out of your mouth. But I will make you dig deeper and go farther, farther than you have ever gone before. You will earn My blessings with an everlasting foundation. America will never leave Me or forget My name again! For I will burn My name, "Jesus Christ," on your thighs in gold so all will know who and what you stand for. Then…then you will be ready, for I will bless you as leaders of the Western world. Once again, people from all nations will dream of the opportunity to come to America. Rejoice on that day America, your fight and endurance will be victorious.

I, Jesus Christ the Mighty, have spoken!"

The New Covenant

This message came to me on August 13, of 2017, concerning the new covenant the Lord made with the Nation of the Cross. The Lord our God said, "Joshua, speak on My behalf about the new covenant, and explain to your people the wonderful blessings I have for them."

My fellow servants, come and see what God has done! Concerning the covenant for America, I must remind you of the scriptures that tell us:

"When the Lord speaks of a new covenant, it means that He has made the first one obsolete. It is now out of date and will soon disappear."

Also, before I speak of the blessings in store for our nation, I must remind you that we must go through a cleansing to the highest degree. We must be ready for all the authority that is about to be given to us. Here is an old saying:

"Sometimes you must serve in order to lead."

And that, my children of God, is exactly what our great and mighty Lord is going to teach us.

When our nation was being forged, the Lord instructed our ancestors to drive out the inhabitants of the land, (Just like when Israel conquered their land under Moses and Joshua), and take possession of what God's grace had made available. The natives, who worshipped mother nature and believed in animal spiritism, erected Asherah poles on every high hill, made idols, and worshipped the sun and all the host of Heaven. But slowly, the Lord led our ancestors to defeat the Huron, Sioux, and Cherokee people. Other tribes like Choctaw, Chippewa, and the Navajo peoples, stood no chance against Jesus Christ and

His Saints. As we took possession of the land, we spread the good news of our King throughout the entire nation, converting many members of these tribes to Christ. This was the great expansion led by France, Britain, and the descendants of Tarshish, (Spain, and Portugal). They sailed in the name of Jesus. And now, as we inch closer to our King's return, He has promised a new American Covenant filled with love and grace.

Now it is faith that will be needed to take the full blessing of this covenant. It is faith that will lead us to new heights never before seen in our nation! It was the faith of our ancestors that made this nation possible. Their faith was as strong as a rock, unmovable. Even in the midst of tyranny, they knew that the Lord was with them. They knew that eventually He would loosen the stranglehold of British rule and give them a country of their own. We will need to find that same faith and courageousness that our ancestors had, which is locked deep within our Spirits. Look upon the Lord with confidence and say! "We will take what the Lord has made available to us! And we will stop at nothing!" C'mon America! We are the leaders!

Encouragement During the Construction of the Covenant

We will fight with pure hearts. Our minds completely focused on the task at hand. No outside motives will be tolerated! Only the will of Jesus Christ our King. This is how we will take our nation to new heights: through the power of the Lord God Almighty and His Holy Spirit. The battle is His; the victory, already won.

Remember how Nehemiah and the returning exiles built the wall, with swords in one hand and a trowel in the other? This is how we will rebuild our nation once again. The Lord is with us; He will never forsake us! This judgment is different from the others because it involves the seven years of terror, followed by the return of the Lord. So we will have to scratch and claw to worship our great God and keep what's left of our country together. But just as Gideon's army marched, the Lord's Army will march ahead of us, claiming victory in the name of Jehovah. Great, miraculous battles will be won without any soldiers taking the field, so we will take no credit in victory, giving all glory to God our Father.

The Remnant of America

A great remnant will rise up during the tribulation, the ones left behind. They will see the truth in our ministry. The Holy Spirit will come upon them with great conviction because our nation is rooted in the fundamentals of God's Word. They will finally realize all that was taught and spoken to them was entirely true, once we are raptured. A great leader will rise up during this terrible time, and the people will follow him. The Lord's hand will be upon him. His very name means "To Honor God." And his people will be protected.

See an army rise, for the name of Jesus has been branded in their hearts. To the King of Kings, they ride out, seeking the will of the Lord. Rise up, army! Rise up! For the victory is at hand! The American Covenant awaits; take it by faith! Your kingdom will last forever!

All will come to worship and make the journey here in the West to one place, and God has given this location to us. Don't you see? All will travel to Jerusalem to worship in the East on the appointed feasts and Passover. But here in the West, a New Jerusalem will be born out of our land, so we can partake of the same appointed feasts and Passover celebrations. Our ancestors called this nation the "New World" and the "New Land." So we will construct a city and name it "New Jerusalem", not to replace the existing Jerusalem, but to add to it. To honor our God. For the Lord is everywhere, don't you see? He will be in the land of Jacob and in our nation simultaneously, so the whole world can worship and give glory to God at one time! Hallelujah! What a glorious blessing! For the mighty Lord Jesus has made a promise to us, that a king will stand at the helm of our nation forever, and his city will be the center of worship in the West. The United States of America and Israel are the two most hated nations on the planet; this is not a coincidence. We share a common bond between us. We are family, and the Lord has made a joining covenant with both nations as leaders.

Don't be discouraged by the judgment of our nation, for it is just, and will make us stronger. Remember, the Lord chastens those He loves. He will purify our nation, so we will be ready to lead. We are Americans! This is our country! The Lord is with us! Lay the foundation of the new covenant for our descendants. We must fight to keep our nation! You say, "The South will rise again." Now is the time! Take it! We are the backbone of our country! Jesus is our name! One team! One fight! No matter what race, what creed, or how we got here! We fight in the name of Jesus! Because we are Jesus! We take His is name at the marriage supper! Therefore, we are one! There is no other name than Jesus! C'mon my countrymen! Dig in and fight! We will be victorious!

Instructions for Fasting

The Holy Spirit is a wonderful gift from the Lord, and many times He will encourage you or prompt you to fast and pray. This can be for yourself, or many times it can be for others. As we go through our daily lives, many decisions or issues come about that are, honestly, too much for us to handle without the Lord's guidance. This could be for someone's healing, a decision in the courts, or possibly moving to a new area. No matter what the cause may be, there are many difficult situations that sometimes call for special prayer and fasting. It seems in recent times that we have gotten away or maybe do not understand fasting. It is a way to deny your flesh and focus more on the Holy Spirit that lives in you. In this way, the Spirit will give insight to the will of God. Sometimes our fallen nature and flesh will have incorrect motives. This can cause problems when we seek our own desires and not the desires of the Lord.

Now fasting doesn't always mean giving up certain foods and drink. This can be anything that you enjoy doing or may be prompted to give up for a period of time; that shows our Father your dependency upon Him and His will. Always follow up fasting with intense prayer. Make a conscious effort to pray about the circumstance or situation earnestly and often during your time of fasting. Our Father hears the prayers of His children, so be diligent. But as Jesus our King stated, make sure to be humble about your fasting and prayer. This is between you and your Father, so do not to make a big spectacle about your fasting. If someone offers you food that you have given up for your fast, kindly tell them the situation and what you are doing. Then they won't be offended. If they seem genuine about your circumstance, ask them to pray for you. Finally, be sure of your motives for fasting. Sometimes we get confused about what we want, instead of what we need. Make sure to keep all selfishness aside. I love you, and may the Lord bless you on your journey.

Instructions for Worship and the Seven Festivals

The Lord said to Joshua, "Record this order for your countrymen who will lead the way when I make My return"

This is what the Lord says:

"These instructions are for New Jerusalem and all nations in the West. Send these letters directly to the chief priest, prophets, and all advisors of the king in New Jerusalem. Timothy, dispatch these messages throughout the land and all places of worship. For these are the seven appointed festivals of worship, in addition to your Sabbath days, that are to take place after I, the Lord your God, make My return. I will send Jacob to come visit your people, so that you both may learn from each other. He will teach you about these festivals, and you will teach him how to worship in the Spirit.

The Three Pilgrimage Festivals

"There are three pilgrimage festivals that must be made every year to New Jerusalem. These are permanent instructions for all generations, as every man must present his family before the Lord.

The Feast of Unleavened Bread (Pesach)

The Feast of Weeks (Pentecost or Shavuot)

The Feast of Tabernacles/Shelters (Sukkot)

"Unlike in times past, when only men made the pilgrimage, you may bring your entire family. Bring all servants with their families. These festivals are to be celebrated with all men, women, and children. All families must make the trip to New Jerusalem and partake in these wonderful festivals to worship the Lord your God and have fellowship with one another. All servants with their families are to partake in the celebration as regular citizens. When arriving at these feasts, you are not to treat your hired help as servants for the entire duration of the festival. After all, they are My children, and I will not tolerate this kind of behavior!

"These festivals are to take place outdoors on the palace grounds in New Jerusalem. These grounds will be designated specifically for the three events every year. No work shall be done, except for those families who are designated to cook for the masses and organize the feast. Each family will take turns on a rotational schedule to work one feast per year. They will help prepare the food and organize the feast with the priest and prophets in New Jerusalem. Make sure each family only works a specific feast once every three years. In this way, no one group will have to work the same feast in consecutive years. Servants with their families will also be in the rotational schedule just as the other families are.

"Prophets, priests, and all leaders throughout New Jerusalem and the Western Provinces: Make sure to enjoy these feasts as well. Do not overwork yourselves. Have a meeting with all elders from each province and tribe when arriving in New Jerusalem. Come together and distribute certain tasks that must be done.

I, the Lord of Heaven's Army, command this. Enjoy yourselves."

Passover, the Feast of Unleavened Bread, and the Festival of First Fruits

"At the appointed time in early spring, all will arrive in New

Jerusalem by evening to celebrate the Lord's Passover with a tremendous feast. This will be a glorious time. All people will be exceedingly glad to come and give thanks to the Lord your God. After that evening's feast is over, the next day will begin the Feast of Unleavened Bread. This will last seven days. All bread will be made without yeast, as no leavened bread will be eaten for the entire seven days. On the first day, a Holy assembly and day of worship will take place on the palace grounds followed by a feast. No regular work shall be done on this day, except for the designated families who are cooking and organizing the festival. On the seventh and final day of the festival, another Holy assembly and day of worship will take place on the palace grounds, followed by a closing feast that evening. Again, no regular work shall be done, except for those families scheduled to cook and organize the festival.

"Two days after Passover, which is the second day of the Feast of Unleavened Bread, will be the Festival of First Fruits. This represents the resurrection of Christ, a most Holy day. Be sure to celebrate this day with worship in the Spirit. Hold a solemn assembly followed by a feast that evening."

The Feast of Weeks

"Count seven weeks from the Feast of First Fruits. This will be the evening before Pentecost, the day the Holy Spirit descended. You are to arrive in New Jerusalem on that forty-ninth day and hold a magnificent feast, followed by a worship ceremony on the palace grounds. The next two days will begin the Feast of Weeks, which will be dedicated to the Lord your God in thanksgiving. No work shall be done, except for those doing the cooking and organization of the celebration. Hold your assemblies at the palace grounds, continuing the tradition that each family will work only once every three years during Pentecost. Leavened bread is acceptable at this feast. This is a time for giving and sacred assemblies. Remember the Spirit that lives in you, for it is Holy."

The Festival of Trumpets (Rosh Hashanah)

"The first of the autumn festivals begins with a blast of trumpets in every town and community throughout the land. This will commemorate all judgments and the Day of the Lord. You will begin to prepare yourselves for the Day of Atonement. This will be a great day of repentance and acknowledgment of the Lord your God's great power. Make sure you celebrate this in your own country and towns with a sacred assembly. No regular work shall be done on this day. Each family shall make a food offering that is pleasing to the Lord and bring it to the feast after the service has ended in your hometowns."

The Day of Atonement (Yom Kippur)

"Nine days after the Festival of Trumpets is the Day of

Atonement, which represents the day the Lord your God, Jesus Christ, paid for your sins once and for all. This is a most Holy day and will be celebrated wherever you live in your own communities. It will begin after supper, the evening before the Day of Atonement, and end the following evening with your community sharing a feast together. This will be a day of heavenly fasting and earnest prayer, giving thanks to the Lord your God, who is the sacrificial lamb. Make sure to have a sacred assembly in your own country and towns. No leavened bread shall be eaten, and no meat of any kind shall be eaten until the evening feast. No regular work shall be done on this day, period! Everyone in the community, including men, must help prepare the feast for that evening. Make sure to do it with love and humility. This is a day to humble yourselves before the Lord. I will come and dine with you that evening, for I love you all so very much.

I, Jesus the Christ, have spoken."

The Feast of Tabernacles

"On the fifth day after the Day of Atonement shall be the Feast of Tabernacles. All will make the trip and arrive in New Jerusalem for seven days. On the first and last day of the festival, you will have great assemblies at the palace grounds. No regular work should be done on the first and last day of the festival, except for those scheduled to cook and organize the feast. In addition to this festival, you must live in tents or shelters for the entire week. This will remind each generation to commemorate how I brought their ancestors up to Me in the rapture, protecting and sheltering My Saints during the great judgment. These seven festivals will be permanent festivals throughout all generations.

I, Jesus Christ the Mighty, have spoken."

Joshua's Final Words

My heart, O how my heart burns with desire of victory, no matter what the cost. My thoughts, consumed with Jesus and my fellow Saints. How I wish I could tear off this body and flesh! I see it! The Lord my God has revealed it to me! I can see it! It's hidden deep within you, my countrymen. That fire is still there. I now understand. I have eaten the Lord's lightning, and am now filled with thunder! By now, after everything that has been revealed, you know what you have to do. Look at one another. Take a good hard look at one another. Believe. . . Believe. . . For the love of our God. . . Believe.

Our nation is destined for greatness. You are destined for greatness. What is your dream? What is that dream that the Lord God Almighty has put in your heart ever since you were young? Remember? Do you remember? It will not go away until you fulfill your destiny. Your time is not over! You're not too old! Go for it! Start today! We have much work to be done! Let's do it together! Follow your dream, and let the Lord guide you in everything! We need you! I know the Lord has a perfect job for you in His army. Believe! He has a job for you that will bring Him glory. And nothing in the universe is more fulfilling than doing the will of God! Go for it! Follow that dream and join us in this fight. C'mon, my Saints! Unite the clans! Unite! Stop the division among us! Remember the covenant! Remember New Jerusalem! Remember what has made our county great! Remember what our ancestors and founding fathers came here for! We are of One Church! One Team! And One Fight! Unite! Return to the Lord! Come and see what God has done!

To Jacob, My Love

This is what your King, Jesus Christ, says:

"Israel, My kingdom, stand up! I am coming! Get ready, for I am sending mighty Angels to protect you. Michael, My general, is raising up an army for your cause. In the warrior's code, there's no surrender! My covenant with you will last forever; I will not forsake you. My Spirit cannot hold back any longer. It must enter you! I will make you strong. You will be an unmovable rock to the other nations. Stand firm! Hold fast! Your King is coming!

"Christians, I have made a fortress for you. My sons and daughters who live in the nations surrounding Jacob, go to him! I will protect you there. Minister to your brother Jacob, cultivate and seed his heart, prepare him for when Moses and Elijah harvest the crop. O Jacob! My Jacob! Look, everyone! My son is coming home!"

Amalgamations

The Kingdom Expands

The Word of the Lord came to Joshua David during the 3rd year of President Trump's reign.

These are the instructions I recorded set forth by the King of Kings:

The Lord said to Joshua, "These instructions are for the new covenant I have made with America. Law and order must be the foundation of this continent, and America will be made the model from which Judah and the rest of the world will be molded when I return. I am counting on you, America, to lead the way once again as we begin the New Age. After the judgment of North America, you will institute this law in New Jerusalem, which will be safely nestled in the hills and mountains of the Cumberland. Your duty is to practice and perfect justice before I return.

"I will send voyagers from Judah to learn from you after I return. This will take place at the beginning of the thousand-year reign of peace. During this time, nations will not be at war with each other; in fact, they will be united by a common bond, as I will dwell with you on Earth. So, this is important; you have big shoes to fill, America. As I said before, I love you more than you will ever know. You have been faithful to Me during this tumultuous time on Earth. I know everything around you is pulling you down, and without My Spirit, you Southern States would be lost. But I have searched your hearts and have found good and pure motives. My Spirit will protect you. It will give you the love, compassion, and steady awareness that are needed during this time of judgment.

"Teach the younger ones all that you can during this time. You will have a small window of opportunity to plant seeds that will root in deep and flourish when the right time comes. Don't worry or get discouraged when the young ones complain and mock you in disbelief. It is My will that they harden their hearts, but these special chosen ones will be the remnant that thrust all nations to become of one mind and one Spirit. You must remember that Judah is going to be like an infant compared to America. My Spirit will rest upon them after I send My two witnesses. You, America, know My Spirit; you know how I operate; your generations have been with Me for centuries! So, it is you who will teach Judah and be a model for him to follow.

Receptiveness Brings Wisdom

"As you know, what I teach is to prepare on Earth as it is in Heaven. I am the Great Teacher, and My students run to Me with eager hearts, ready to listen to what I have to say. Today, My children, I need you to become students. Remember, I cannot teach you heavenly things if you've put up walls and have closed your heart for new beginnings. I am always busy creating projects for new beginnings with new perceptions. I am the Creator, and I will never stop building and creating to make everything better for My children and I. I have made Saints and Angels in the same image as the Trinity. You are just like Me! You are My children. A son is like his father, and a daughter will always be Daddy's little girl. So just like your Heavenly Father, who is the King, you are all princes and princesses who love to build and create with your hands.

"You cannot rest without a purpose; think about this. What is rest without striving for a goal? After a hard day's work, do you not like to stop, rest, and look at what you have built and worked so hard for? The Sabbath is for worship and fellowship, yes, but it is also a time for rest and for enjoying the fruit of your labors. It is good to have purpose and goals. Yes, I will give you rest here in the 3rd Heaven, but you will always have a purpose and strive to make things better and want more. It's in your nature to want more, because you come from My loins. Ask yourselves, why are Angels so eager to go out and do the Lord's work, leaving the 3rd Heaven? Solomon was the wisest of all men on Earth, and yet he was never satisfied, even though his kingdom was the greatest that Earth has ever seen. I am this way as well; this is why Saints and Angels always strive for new goals and new adventures.

Setting the Courts

"We will now turn to judges and the system of the courts. As we have court in Heaven, you also have court on Earth. Because everything that leaves the 3rd Heaven is subject to sin, we must have justice and order. We not only have court in Heaven for what takes place on Earth, but we also have court for what takes place in the 2nd Heaven as well. As soon as Angels leave My presence and enter the 2nd Heaven to do My work, they are subject to sin just as you are. Angels are far from perfect just like you Saints. Therefore, I must represent and defend them just as I defend you. You are all My children. I love you all, and not one of you is more important than the other. We are all joined by the Holy Spirit, making us family. It brings Me joy to be one with Angels and Saints through My Spirit. As I said before, whoever does the will of God is My brother, sister, and mother, whether that be Angel or man.

"But our focus is on Earth for the moment. So let's get started, shall we? In New Jerusalem you will have a king, and he will be the Supreme Court judge. Just as Moses received godly advice from his father-in-law, Jethro, the king will appoint judges to assist him—men and women who are God fearing and trustworthy, and who seek justice and hate what is evil; citizens who love the Lord with all their heart, and who seek My will and hate dishonest gain. The king will survey the towns and cities throughout the land and appoint these citizens personally. Do not be surprised if the king and his officials appoint prophets and high priests in your towns to be judges. After all, he is seeking men and women who have the respect of the people to do what is just and right. Priests and prophets serve the Lord their God day and night, and they should be trusted as honorable individuals.

"There are to be three judges per town or province. The king and his council will appoint two judges; the third judge will be voted in by the people of the town or province. In this way, the citizens will appoint a trustworthy and reliable man or woman whom they know personally to become their judge. After this, if a judge must step down due to sickness or retirement, or has passed away, the town or province must vote on who will replace the former one. These judges will handle simple cases that come up in the town or provinces in which you live—cases they feel they can handle and are led by the Lord to take care of. You will send difficult cases, or cases that require the Supreme Court, to New Jerusalem to be handled by the king and the other Supreme Court judges.

"Listen to your Father: A court system must remain in place during the millennial reign because all men and women have the curse of Adam. That is, you have a fallen nature, and some sins of the flesh are unavoidable. The tempter and accuser will be locked in prison, yes, but you cannot hide from your earthly bodies.

I, the Lord God Almighty, have spoken."

Supreme Court Judges

The Lord said to Joshua:

"Supreme Court judges will be selected by King Timothy in New Jerusalem when the millennial reign begins. These courts will be held in New Jerusalem. There will be seven Supreme Court judges at all times. Timothy will select six Supreme Court judges to assist him as a judge. The king of New Jerusalem will forever hold one position as a Supreme Court judge. After Timothy's selections, if a judge must step down due to sickness or retirement, or in the event of death, you must hold a vote to replace that judge. From that point on, the public will vote on all selections for Supreme Court judges. Citizens of New Jerusalem and all towns and provinces across the country will participate in this vote. Current judges in other towns and provinces may apply for this position. Qualified candidates for the position will be made available for the king and his officials to review. Once the board reviews have been made, the public will vote on the candidates for the position. This will distribute some of the king's power. These seven judges will collectively handle the day-to-day cases specifically for New Jerusalem, as well as hold Supreme Court hearings one day per week. No court shall be in session throughout the entire nation on or during the seven Holy festivals, including the Sabbath day!"

Regulations and Governing Laws

"Laws and regulations throughout New Jerusalem and laws that are made nationwide shall be voted on by the Supreme Court judges. All seven Supreme Court judges will vote. A regulation or law will either pass or be rejected by a minimum four-to-three margin vote. The laws that are passed will be made permanent throughout the entire nation, as well as any laws that are rescinded. National laws cannot be rescinded or passed in any other way except by the Supreme Court.

"However, if a town or province would like to make additional laws to govern locally, it may do so as long as the law does not interfere with any national laws. A town or province may do so by having the three judges vote on the matter. The law will either be accepted or rejected by a minimum two-to-three margin vote. Presenting a law to be added or rescinded nationally will require a petition signed by judges from multiple provinces and towns. Then the Supreme Court will review and vote on it. Presenting laws to be added or rescinded for a specific town or province will require petitions signed by the majority of the citizens who live in that town or province.

"Make laws and regulations that are morally sound in your Spirit. I am with you, My children. I will guide your steps and make sure that you make good decisions. You are My special people, and it excites Me that America is going to lead the way during the New Age. I, the Lord your God, love you so very much."

Rules for Judges

"I, the Lord, appoint judges and set up government for good reason. And I give all authority over to whom I choose. For this purpose, you shall obey those who have authority over you. A ranking officer is in that position for a reason, and you shall follow orders regardless of what you may or may not agree with. Just as Angels follow orders in rank, so shall you Saints follow orders. And when I bring you up to Me, Saints and Angels will work together as one unit with each of you having certain authority and rank. You have read the scriptures that state some of you Saints will judge Angels; likewise, some Angels will judge you Saints. I give all authority to whomever I deem fit and ready for that authority.

"When I put someone in a position of high authority, such as a judge, too much I have given, much will be required. These requirements include that judges rule with confidence but also with compassion. A judge must be just, use good moral judgment, and hate evil, but also have a forgiving heart. Judges should not become crowd-pleasers or become boastful of their position, lest they become prideful. A judge should not take sides but evaluate a case objectively, without prejudice. Judges should not be involved in greedy business or property deals. This may skew their judgment on certain cases. They should also never take bribes or be involved in secret meetings. I despise these acts! I am holding you judges accountable personally and have set you at a higher standard. Therefore, be on alert and quick to please the Lord in all that you do. Integrity is the key to your success. If your integrity is lost and the citizens have no faith in your justice, you will be stripped of your power. So keep a watchful eye on yourselves, trust the Holy Spirit, and be mindful of your intentions and fleshly impulses. Remember, as judges, you have the power to give and to take away miracles. I pray that your love and compassion will inspire you to give them.

I, the Lord Jesus Christ, have spoken."

Supreme Court Instructions for Seeking the Lord

The Lord continues to instruct Joshua:

"For difficult cases in the Supreme Court, take a one-day recess to seek the Lord's will. Pray earnestly, and fast if need be to seek the Lord your God. If the king is not a prophet, and most kings will not be, he must seek the counsel of a prophet of the Lord in New Jerusalem. These prophets will be designated by the king for this duty. There will be a minimum of three prophets designated for the courts, preferably more but no less than three. These prophets will be on a rotational schedule known only to the king and the other Supreme Court judges. In this way, the public and people from outside towns will not know which prophet is assigned to the next case. This will ensure that no corruption, bribery, or outside influence will sway the prophet's decision. The prophet will then relay the decision to the king, and the court shall resume the following day. If the prophet has not made a decision and is still waiting for a message from the Lord, by all means take an additional two days. If by the third day the prophet still has not received a message from the Lord, then the Lord is trusting in the prophet's judgment on what must take place."

Women in the Court

"There will be times when I will command a prophet or priest to appoint certain women as judges to be voted in. Therefore, do not become dismayed or surprised when this takes place. Some of My daughters make better judges than most men, and there are times when certain cases need a woman's touch. If one of My daughters has a gift to become a trustworthy judge, do I not use that gift? After all, I gave her this quality, and to not use this gift would be gluttonous. In some of your towns, there will be women who are in leadership positions. This is the will of your Father, and I will not stand for any of My daughters to be treated as second-class citizens or slaves simply because they are women. I, Jesus Christ, command this! Now use good judgment, and you will find that what I have said is good."

Women Priests and Prophets

"This brings Me to women priests and women prophets. As you know in the scriptures, I have raised up women who became My prophets, and I will continue to always do so. Prophets are intercessors for My will and have been trained spiritually for this task. All of My children have the qualities of a prophet because My Spirit dwells within them, but there are some whom I choose to become more active in this gift. To see the prophet or seer is to seek the Lord's guidance and will. This may be a woman or a man.

"Now for women priests: I may call or choose a woman to become a priest. She should study under the leading priests and prophets and become a woman of God. She may become their assistant, teach My Word to the public, and give godly advice. A woman should never be the leading priest of a town or province. However, in the event that something happens to the leading priest in a town or province, a woman can act as the leading priest until another priest is appointed or anointed. Do not rush this process or become frantic; in due time one will be appointed. I expect support for the women during this time of transition."

Outside Judges

"There will be times when certain towns or provinces may need to call upon judges in neighboring towns. Judges should be quick to assist and help other towns that may be in need or may not have judges in place yet. This pleases the Lord your God. In cases that involve a current judge's family member or business partner, or any pertinent reason an opposing party feels he or she cannot get a fair trial, the court must pursue an outside judge in a neighboring town. Because the current judge has been compromised due to extenuating circumstances, this will ensure that the outside judge will be unbiased toward the case."

Dismissal of Judges

"If a judge has sinned in a way that has destroyed the public's trust, has become unreasonable to work with, or lacks the mental capacity to continue as a judge but refuses to step down, the current judges of that town or province must make a declaration with backing evidence. They must present this evidence to the Supreme Court for a ruling. The Supreme Court will determine if a judge has been ruled unfit for service, and that judge will be relieved of his or her duties if found guilty or mentally unstable.

"For matters that involve the removal of a Supreme Court judge, all seven judges must have a private meeting. Six judges need to be unanimous in their decision for a Supreme Court judge to step down; this includes the king who holds a seat in the Supreme Court. If the king has been forced to step down as a judge, his successor must be put in place as a Supreme Court judge. If the king has no sons to succeed him as judge, and his grandson is not of serviceable age, the king's daughter will be appointed as judge on the Supreme Court until the firstborn son is ready and available for that position. The queen shall rule as Supreme Court judge if no daughters, sons, or grandsons are of serviceable age. A judge should be thirty years of age or older, but I understand when there are circumstances in which this cannot take place.

As judges grow old, they may hold on to their positions for too long. So remember, you are working for the people. Do what is good and in the best interest of the citizens, not your own. As public servants to the highest degree, I hold you judges responsible for the trajectory of your country."

Representatives

"Complainants or defendants may have a representative to assist them in presenting a case to the judge. Some cases will involve minors or those with special needs who are unable to represent themselves. Therefore, they will need assistance in this matter. A party looking for a professional to represent an argument before the courts is also permitted. These representatives, if possible, can come to an agreement with both parties and present that agreement to the judge for a final ruling. In this way, most arguments can be resolved reasonably, with the representatives acting as mediators for the parties.

"In the courts of Heaven, I defend and represent you because you are citizens of the 3rd Heaven. Even though you're not present to defend yourselves, I have assigned representatives and set up a council on your behalf to present your case. Representatives should be honest and work for their clients. They should not take bribes or be swayed by the public's opinion. This command also pertains to all judges. Judges and representatives work for the people to maintain peace and justice. You are appointed to these positions because of your integrity and your reputation for being fair and honest. To lose these virtues is to lose your credibility in these positions."

A Message to Australia

This message concerning Australia came to Joshua on October 25, 2018.

This is what the Lord says:

"Do not think I have forgotten you, my sweet children. I have big plans for you as well. I have never forgotten what you did during the 1st World War. What you did for the Aramean Saints was unprecedented. You have flourished during this last century and have become close friends with the Americans. I have seen the way you have kept My Word, and for that I am ready to bless your nation with a new covenant. Now listen, my Aussie children, a great multitude of Saints will rise up out of the tribulation in your country. Your little brother, New Zealand, will lean on you during this time. Take him into your home and comfort him. Give him clothes and allow him to live among you. You two brothers will lead your continent into the New Age. I will make your nation great during the millennial age and see to it that you are well taken care of. Stay close to the Americans for you will learn much from them, as I have made a similar covenant with you. I will have your ambassadors set sail with my beloved Jacob, so that both of your kings and officials will meet on American soil. There you will make a solemn pact with each other in front of the Lord your God. You three nations will make an everlasting covenant with each other. Celebrate this day every year in your nations. For this will be a day of Thanksgiving, the day three separate nations became one. You will be My people, and I will add each of you into the Kingdoms of Heaven. You will look upon each other as David looked upon his best friend, Jonathan. The three of you will become as one, and nothing will separate the love we have for one another. I will never forsake you.

I, Jesus Christ the Mighty have spoken!"

1 Gentiles

I am writing this letter to Timothy, my chosen son. I write to my son who has not yet been born. Yet, the Lord my God has promised and decreed that a child from my loins be named Timothy, that he will rule as king at the dawn of the millennial reign. He has made a new covenant with you and I, young Timothy! For your name will shine greatly during the tribulation period. The Lord has put His hand upon you in a miraculous way.

Who are we, Timothy, to be so favored by the Lord and receive such unwarranted blessings from our Father? What have we to offer the Mighty One? I search myself weekly, and in my opinion, I come up short every time. I'm so thankful that the Lord doesn't look at me in the same way I do of myself. I could do so much more for Him. But we cannot go around condemning ourselves. I've learned that man can go around beating themselves up better than Satan ever could. Mistakes are compounded by self-loathing and unforgiveness of our own actions.

Timothy; don't waste your time thinking this way. It is not healthy, nor does it produce the correct fruit that our Father desires. If we are focused on ourselves and constantly worrying about what we might say or do to foul things up, then we cannot operate out of the Spirit. In fact, we are operating out of fear and selfishness. If we operate out of fear, then we will be limited to the blessings that God has in store for us. We are not perfect, and the Lord has accounted for this. He knows what we will do before we even do it. So when you make a mistake, or when your tongue gets you into trouble, don't sulk over it again and again in your mind. You are creating a door for Satan to use by stirring up condemning thoughts of yourself.

Strength in the Valleys

As God brings us through life to prepare us for what our calling, our dream, and His purpose is on our lives, we must expect valleys. Valleys can be long and dry, seeming as if you will never receive what the Lord has promised. You may feel that you will never conquer the valley, or that you're not supposed to, causing you to lose heart and become frustrated. It is in the valley that God builds our character: how we react when everything around us has failed, what you do and how you respond when you're poor, how you live your life when you have nothing to offer the Lord other than your time. This is what brings forth the correct fruit and the type of person God has called you to be. This is how God trains us to listen to the Spirit, not the flesh. During these times, we hear God's voice but want to disobey because nothing seems to be happening. It's as if the Lord has forgotten us, and we start to doubt all that the Lord has promised. Even worse, you start to doubt the mission the Lord has called you to do. Those are the times when you must dig in! Dig in a little deeper, trusting what the Lord has promised. The enemy wants you to get discouraged and quit because he knows that is the only way to stop you. But you're not a quitter, Timothy! Honor the Lord during the struggle; honor Him during the bad times! Remember, Christ suffered the most grueling mission and gruesome death for us, but in everything He went through, He honored our Heavenly Father.

Some people can't handle the valleys, but you, Timothy, you can handle the valley. You're strong and courageous, and you lead by example. The Lord wouldn't have chosen you if He didn't think you could handle it. So even when it seems all hope is lost or when you make that big mistake, remember the Lord is with you. Keep pressing forward and doing the right thing. Don't meditate on what you did wrong or how bad your situation is. Keep your mind on the vision God gave you. Remember that all of Heaven is counting on you to do God's will for His people. Heaven is praying and rooting for you to add to our Father's Kingdom. Remember that what you do is for your countrymen, not yourself. When you want to raise your fist at God, shouting at Him for choosing you for this task, or when you plead with the Lord to pick someone else and tell Him that you didn't ask for this mission, remember the love you have for the people. These are your citizens, and you are their king. Let your service for the people thrust you forward, just as Moses did through the wilderness. In the end, Moses wasn't inspired or motivated by the Lord to bring his people to the promised land. Moses loved the people of

Israel so much that he felt obligated to complete his mission and purpose for the Israelites. It was love for the people that propelled and motivated Moses to victory.

Remember Who You Are in Christ

Timothy, do not get lost in what your function is for the Kingdom of God. You're a soldier! Most of the time, you're not going to act like a priest. So don't get bent out of shape because you're not living your life like a pastor or priest who runs a church or place of worship. The Lord did not call you to be a full-time pastor, just as He did not with me. You're just like me, Timothy, and the Lord wants you to be a little rough around the edges. You exemplify a sinner in this world who needs Christ, and you relate to people on their level. When people look at you as a brother and one of their own, when you can meet people where they are in life, it helps make them more comfortable and not intimidated. Your history and background does this. Knowing that you're not perfect, and that you get your hands dirty with them as a soldier, gains the respect and dignity of your men. Just as King David, the prophet Samuel, and Joshua went out with their troops into battle, so have you and I. Be yourself, and don't be someone you're not. Yes, you are a prophet, Timothy, but you are a soldier prophet, not a priestly prophet. Talk to our Seraphim brothers; they will show you what soldier prophets are and what they are not. I think you will find a connection with them and feel at home.

Controlling the Flesh

Something that the enemy cannot duplicate—the most difficult of all challenges and mistakes that eat away at our soul—is none other than sins of the flesh. They never go away. You cannot defeat this enemy because it lives within you. It is a constant battle that takes discipline and discernment. There are two voices that we constantly hear as Saints in these bodies: one is the Holy Spirit that lives in you, the other is your inner self.

At times the Lord may reveal to you that what you are doing, or a decision that you're about to make, is actually a fleshly action or reaction. We cannot always tell the difference. Refraining from these choices or impulse actions can literally take all that you have. We don't always have time to fast and pray about our circumstances. Remember when Joseph had to run away from Potiphar's wife? Joseph's flesh was at war within himself for months. This woman consistently tried to seduce him. Instinct and carnal nature would have had Joseph having sexual relations with Potiphar's wife, but Joseph fought this instinct and fleshly desire with the only way he physically could. This was to literally run the other way. He knew if he stayed any longer, his flesh would have gotten the best of him. Not all fleshly impulses are this challenging, but we need to identify our nature for what it is. So as our Father in Heaven teaches you to discern between His will and your nature, be sure to take in all that He is trying to inform you of.

Governors and Expanding Provinces

This message came to Joshua from the Lord informing King Timothy of commands and instructions he is to accomplish.

This is what the Lord says:

"Be sure to appoint governors in the many provinces throughout your land. These governors should rule in the provinces as you do from New Jerusalem. They will endorse your policies and commands. These governors and provinces will be subject to you. So rule mightily, but with a loving heart. I will move a great multitude of Latin Americans into your land. They are remnant just as you and your people are. I will bring them up from as far south as Chile and Argentina, up through Panama and into Northern Mexico. Now listen, Timothy; I have given them land in your nation as a reward for their war and efforts for My sake during the tribulation period. They have rededicated themselves to Me and have been My heart over the past seven years. I have promised them land and to join your nation. They are being grafted into this covenant with your people, just as I grafted you Gentiles into Abraham's Covenant. The Latin nations to the South will live among you, and I will give them peace and rest. Be sure to warmly welcome the fleets of Tarshish and his descendants when they arrive on your Carolina shores, for they have been at war helping Brussels in Europe, but they long to return home and reunite on American soil.

"Timothy, you will receive land in Northern Mexico that will be added to your kingdom, from Sonora on the Pacific to as far East as Tamaulipas on the coast. You and your people will continue to vacation in these lands and on the Yucatan Peninsula. I have promised the descendants of Tarshish all of this land, including parts of Texas, Arizona, and up through the Utah country into Colorado. Set this land aside for your Latin brothers, learn their language, and appoint governors for their provinces. I command that El Paso and Juarez, along with Mexico City, be uninhabited for seventy years because of the evil that has ruined the land. It must be cleansed thoroughly before I will have My children live in such wicked places.

"These people are your brothers and sisters; do not treat them as outsiders. Allow them to live and marry among your people. After all, you are all Americans. Your ancestors have come from all over the world. This is why I have made America so great.

I, Jesus Christ the Mighty, have spoken."

The Lord's Line of Wrath

This message came to Joshua David from the Lord concerning the terrible forest fires that ravaged the West Coast for six months during the summer of 2018.

This is what the Lord says:

"I will map out the destruction I am about to release on the West Coast. Fire spews on the land from My mouth year after year, yet you still do not heed My warning. Each year the fires get worse and worse, but you are stubborn people who shake your fist at Me in defiance.

"Is there a more wretched place in this nation? I cannot find one. You have cut yourself off from this nation. You will not receive any blessings on your land as we approach the New Covenant I have made with America. In fact, I will completely destroy the land near the West Coast so that no one can be infected by its disease any longer.

"The area from Tijuana and San Diego across the Mojave wilderness and up through Las Vegas will be a wasteland. Screams of terror will be heard across the Funeral Mountains into Bakersfield and up through Sacramento. I will then continue My campaign through Lake Tahoe and over to Reno, destroying everything in its path. After crossing over the Plumas wilderness, I will pause at Redding. Then I will send My wrath due North, straight through Portland, up to Seattle, and over to Vancouver.

"Everything West of this line will be in utter ruin. The bodies will be laid in Death Valley due to disease and the horrid stench. This land will lie desolate for seventy years so that I may cleanse it. During the end of Timothy's reign, I will reopen these lands as the remnant repopulate and move West from New Jerusalem and the land promised to the descendants of Tarshish.

I, Jesus Christ the Mighty, have spoken!"

Building the Palace

As you know, Timothy, the building and structure that I have made is not fit for a king, let alone the King of Kings, who by now has made His dwelling place here on Earth. So, one of your first tasks will be to build a palace suitable for you and the Lord Jesus Christ when He comes to visit. This palace should be magnificently splendid compared to any and all other buildings. I pray that you make this palace so majestic that even the jaw of Jesus will drop when He comes through the mountains and sees the palace from a distance. Do not forget about the three pilgrimage feast every year. All of America will come to New Jerusalem for worship, fellowship, and celebration on the palace grounds. O' Timothy, *please* do a good job on the palace grounds, my son. Make the grounds better than I can imagine them in my dreams—stages upon stages for worship and song, beautiful decorations, and flowers for the whole world to see. Israel and Australia will be coming to America to explore and examine how to worship and celebrate these awesome feasts during your first few years as king. Show them, Timothy; be the pioneer for the whole world to see and do something special when King Jesus visits our palace every year.

This is very important to me, so please listen to my one and only request: When building the palace for you, your concubine, and all of your officials, make sure that the top room and penthouse suite goes to King Jesus Christ. His room should be the greatest room in the palace, the highest and most luxurious—a room worthy of the King of Kings. Your room should be underneath His on the next floor down. This will honor our

King when He comes to visit. After all, this is His palace, not ours. O and one more request if I may—I know I said one, but I have two: Make two beautiful, spacious rooms with wonderful views on the same floor as your own. Designate these rooms for the King of Israel and the King of Australia when they come to visit. Treat their families as your own, and make them feel at home. You are not above these kings, Timothy. You are just a steward of what the Lord has given you here in America. I love you so much, my son. Godspeed. And remember, I will always be with you and praying for you in spirit.

The Lord's Charge to Timothy

The Lord gave this message to Timothy:

"Timothy, as I was with your father, Joshua, I will be with you. For your father gave his heart to Me and obeyed all My commands with the best of his knowledge. I promised your father, Joshua, this: 'there will always be a descendant in your line who sits on the throne in America.'

"If you will follow all of My decrees and commands, if you live for Me, Timothy, I will make your dynasty the greatest that Earth has ever seen. I will bless you with descendants as numerous as the sand on the seashore. I love your father, and I will always be with you in the same way. I will make sure you honor him and Me in a way that fills your heart with joy.

"Now, for the first command I give you as king:

"You have heard the promise I gave to your Latin American brothers to the South. You are to treat them as your own, learn their language, and allow them to settle among you and intermarry among your people. Your people, along with Tarshish, are descendants of Japheth, the great seafaring people of the West. I have blessed Japheth's descendants greatly and will continue to do so, but Javen and his son Tarshish have fallen in love with idols. They have allowed Jezebel to infiltrate their worship. And this I cannot allow.

"You must rid them of all their idols. Destroy every single one! Many of them will have repented of this practice during the tribulation and understand completely, but there are some who are rooted too deeply into this worship, including some of your own people. Mary is here with Me in Heaven, and at no time has she ever asked or wanted to be worshipped! You worship the Trinity and Us only! Just as she does.

"If you do not get rid of all idols throughout your land, I will cause them to be a thorn in your side for as long as you rule. They will cause your people to sin, and I will be forced to punish America for her fornication. I will have no choice but to uproot and scatter her across the world. We have been down this path before; learn from the mistakes of Jacob. Destroy all of the idols! Set the example high, Timothy. It is your nation that all other nations will turn to for guidance. I know your father is praying for your wisdom as I write to you this very moment. Be strong and courageous, My son, for I, your Heavenly Father, loves you and will be with you always."

2 Gentiles

This letter is from Joshua David, the protector of Saints, whom the Lord chose to fulfill His will. I am writing to the Gentiles across the nations and to my brother, Jacob. It is time to reveal one of the great mysteries, for the Lord has ravaged me with tormenting and wrathful spirits so that I may feel His anger. Fear the Lord and Him only, for He is the Mighty One who controls all things.

The Emergence

Since the flood and the emergence of Cush, the king of Shinar, you Gentiles have fallen in love with pagan gods and pagan rituals, set up idols, and made graven images. In an attempt to exclude the Creator from all forms of recognition and judgment, Nimrod built large cities and high towers after leaving the high ground, trying to eliminate another deluge and suppress the population into relying on large government with different acts of tyranny. As Nimrod's mother, Semiramis, exclaimed after the death of his father, Cush:

"I sit enthroned as Queen. I am no helpless widow! And never shall I see mourning!"

Semiramis enticed and seduced her own son to lie in bed with her, giving his hand in marriage to his mother. She then instituted polytheism into a worldly religion, and so the Babylonian system began. It then spread once God scattered the people across Earth and gave them different languages. The same system was in place, just with different names for their gods. For the Great Harlot, who sits on many waters, spreads her legs for all, man or Angel.

All of these practices are detestable to the Lord our God. Our Father created the Hebrew people from Abraham's loins, moving Abraham from the city of Ur in Shinar to Canaan in hopes of sheltering his descendants from the works of the Great Harlot and the disobedient Sons of God. However, we have learned that the Israelites still continued to intermarry and join in the many sins of the nation's surrounding them.

The flesh can cause some of God's greatest creations to sin and become blind to the will of our Father. Humans, along with Angels who live in earthly bodies, tend to justify sins and compromise decisions to please the flesh at times. These choices have irreversible consequences. After all, the Lord has given us free will, but with that comes conviction and discernment from the Holy Spirit.

Appointing Priests and Prophets

Do not fall into the same trap as Jeroboam, son of Nebat. For Jeroboam followed the Canaanites, the Hittites, and the

Philistines in the worship of Baal and the Queen of Heaven. He set up shrines and appointed his own priest and prophets in the temples of Baal. Then, as his pride and arrogance grew, he even promoted his own people to become his priest and prophets in the Lord's temples and places of worship. The Lord appoints His men and women for these positions! Never should a king appoint a priest or prophet to a position of this authority! This is a calling by the Lord, and they are chosen by Him to be His representatives. They are to lead in worship, teach the Holy scriptures, and reveal the will of the Lord for certain situations. Isn't it the Lord's business to confirm and establish a prophet? Who is the king to decide whether someone is a prophet or not? This is a gift from the Holy Spirit, and only He gives these gifts! One should not be thrusted into a position of this magnitude unless chosen by the Lord. A king who appoints his own prophets and priest looks to control citizens and use his power for evil. They are the Lord's ambassadors, not the king's!

The Lord's Anger at the Watchmen

Fire comes from the Holy One as He speaks; His eyes are as a blazing furnace.

Hear the wrath of the Lord:

"My anger boils at you, Watchmen! You have disgraced everything that you once stood for. You asked and prayed, without ceasing to be sent down to Earth, to watch and care for the

Saints and what I created. Then you do something deplorable like this! How dare you corrupt all that is Holy! Your wickedness and lust for women has consumed your every thought. Have you not pleased your flesh enough? Must you lavish and gorge yourself on every sexual desire? Your thoughts are increasingly evil.

"You have been cut off from all salvation! You've made your choice and revel in it. Flesh has become your master, as you cannot please your cravings. You've taken the daughters of men and made them your god! Look how the mammoth sits and gazes into her eyes. He is paralyzed by her beauty; he is quick to jump and perform every task and desire that comes from her lips. An evil spell possesses you. The Great Harlot controls everything you do! I sent the floods because of the sickness and disease that you spread on Earth. Man hated Me because of what you Watchmen did! You stole their women! You shamed both men and women publicly! The natural order has been cursed by your fornications! You created a rift that could not be mended. Man waxed exceedingly in anger, shaking their fists as to blame Me for sending you behemoths. Man despised their Heavenly Father and proclaimed war on us both. I regretted even creating man because of what you watchmen did! How could you do this to Me? Why did you do this? I don't understand! You have fallen from grace, and I have mourned long enough for your actions. Once some things are done, they cannot be undone.

"Then you make love with that whore from Babylon and fill her mind with wondering thoughts. Like Samson, you've lain in bed with Semiramis and told her all of your weaknesses.

She has cut your hair, and now all your power is gone. My Spirit no longer resides in you. So is this how you repay Me? Unbelievable! I warned you of the power of sin once you leave the 3rd Heaven. Look at what you all have become! How far will you fall? Satan has filled your hearts with darkness, and now We no longer allow your cases to be heard in the Courts of Heaven. Your judgment is sealed in My books.

"Because My Spirit has left you and Earth is now your home, you have become vengeful and uncontrollable. I have given you what you have lusted over so dearly. It is insulting the way you have spit in My face by creating these jackals, wolves, and beasts. I have spent centuries killing your offspring! And to make matters worse, you behemoths have collaborated with the dragon and coerced him to make love to that whore Semiramis. And now Apollyon sits as king. He has been given his own kingdom in Hades. He makes the bottomless pit his home. Mecca is the center of his abominations. But I have set a trap for the dragon. His hate and pride will be used against him, and he will give all his power over to his son. I will weaken the dragon, constricting his domain to only that of Earth, which is the planet he despised most all along.

I, the Lord of Heaven's Armies, have spoken!"

Death to the Christmas Tree

You have heard the words of the prophet Jeremiah, yet all of Christianity is infatuated with the whore of Babylon!

Let's review, Saints:

Idolatry Brings Destruction

10 1 Hear the word which the Lord speaks to you,
O house of Israel!
Thus says the Lord:
2 "Do not learn the way of the Gentiles (pagan nations);
Do not be terrified and distressed at the signs of Heaven,
For the Gentile nations are terrified by them.
<u>**3** For the customs of the peoples *are* futile;</u>
<u>For *one* cuts a tree from the forest,</u>
<u>The work of the hands of the workman, with the ax or cutting tool.</u>
<u>**4** They decorate it with silver and gold;</u>
<u>They fasten it with nails and hammers</u>
<u>So that it will not topple.</u>
<u>**5** They *are* upright, like a palm tree,</u>
<u>And they cannot speak;</u>
They must be carried,
Because they cannot go *by themselves*.
Do not be afraid of them,
For they cannot do evil,
Nor can they do any good."

This is a command from the Lord!

Have you not seen the Harlot step down the flight of stairs from the 1st Heaven? She makes her nest in the clouds. Her talons encompass the entire planet. She proclaimed herself as the Queen of Heaven after whoring herself out to every Angel and man she could entice. As a medium who feeds all of the dead birds of the sky, she delights in being called the "Mother of Nature" and becomes aroused when Saints and Angels feed on her breast. She is the master of souls who love this planet and the mistress of death. As an Angel she came to Earth in human form and immediately sinned, she defied the Lord without even giving a second thought to her actions, giving birth to her lust and fornication with all the Earth. Instituting the worship of herself, her offspring, and all she makes love to.

She celebrates the resurrection of Nimrod through Tammuz as she opened her legs up for the dragon. It is the pine tree decked and adorned with presents that Semiramis created as an idol, signifying the death and resurrection of the Antichrist! Nimrod was her son, whom she fornicated with through adultery, then later married. Nimrod's death brought forth an evil opportunity, and a beastly son was born of a whore, opposite of the virgin birth. This beast was born from the dragon's seed, who is the king of the bottomless pit, Abaddon.

My Father hates the Christmas tree, as do I! You must destroy this practice. The entire planet has been corrupted by this false Babylonian system. December 25th was celebrated as a day of the resurrected Nimrod in the form of Satan's son Abaddon (Tammuz), whether the pagan nations realized it or not. The Lord scattered all of Babel throughout Earth and gave them different languages, but the system remained. The Roman Catholic Church tried to combat this day centuries

WAKE UP FROM THE INSIDE | 189

ago; in an attempt to honor Jesus Christ and the Virgin Mary, they replaced the Great Harlot Semiramis and the false resurrection of Nimrod through her son Apollyon (Abaddon in Greek). But what followed was a blended version of the two in the worship of Mary and idols. The Catholics' heart was good, but they inadvertently opened the door for Jezebel to infiltrate the Church. The Great Harlot forms her tree and extends her branches to those like Jezebel, Delilah, and Athaliah. Learn from this, my Saints! The Babylonian system is not based on love; it is based on performance and justice. Our Heavenly Father bases His entire covenant system on His love for us Saints and Angels. Those who have the Holy Spirit are all His children, and we are praying that you start a clean slate to build upon when our King arrives on Earth. Don't let Him see this, my Saints.

Instructions for December/Hanukkah

The Lord stands from His throne and addresses the Gentiles:

"I have seen from My Holy mountain the customs of the Gentiles during December. Because of the deep roots involved with this month, it has forced Me to reevaluate the situation at hand. After further review, I have seen much good come out of what was meant to be blasphemous. Celebrating the birth of My son is a good thing. What makes My spirit sing is this tremendous spirit of giving that you Gentiles have. It is truly a gift, and I have blessed this month because I wish to see My children be full of joy and thankfulness. So

I have decreed that from now on December will be a month of giving. It will be a month to acknowledge the virgin birth of My son, Jesus. This will be a month of offerings. During this month, each person shall present an offering to the Lord by doing something out of love and giving their time to serve others. There is nothing you can do that is more valuable and dearer to My heart. This should not be a one-day holiday. This should be the spirit throughout the entire month.

"As you know, I am in the business of uniting all of My children into one, making My kingdom whole. The Jewish people celebrate Hanukkah in remembrance of the 2nd temple being restored, for the miracle I performed in lighting the menorah, and to celebrate rededicating themselves to their Father in Heaven. These are all good things. These eight days during Kislev are the Holy Festival of Lights. And from this point forward, we will combine the two holidays into one, making all Jews and Gentiles whole. You will celebrate this festival together beginning on the 25th day of Kislev in remembrance of the birth of My Son, the Messiah, Jesus Christ. Giving of presents and special offerings to others during these eight days is permitted and should be done with a full heart. Remember, the most important part of this season is the birth of Christ and dedicating yourselves to Him.

"Jacob, I love you so much, and I want you to continue this tradition, but now, since you have come alive in the Spirit, and your eyes are now open to the Messiah, celebrate it with passion for your Judean King Jesus. In this way you Gentiles and Jews will be as one celebrating this festival together in the same fashion. Visit with each other during these eight days and throughout the month, learn each other's customs, and become as family. I love you all so much, and I don't want to take something away that you all love so dearly. I see the good that can come out of it, and I want to celebrate it with you. From this point forward, I decree that this occasion be called the Festival of Lights, for My son Jesus is the light that will shine for all to see forever and ever. Decorate your entire towns and homes with lights. Do not, however, set up an Asherah from the forest inside your homes! Be mindful of what you are celebrating and become one in Spirit.

I, the Lord your God, the God of Abraham, Isaac, and Jacob, have spoken!"

3 Gentiles

Greetings from Joshua David, the protector of Saints. This letter is written for the Gentile nations abroad in Europe. The Lord loves you deeply, and He is ready to inform you of His plan going forward and into the millennial reign.

A Message to Brussels

This message came to Joshua from the Lord concerning Belgium.

This is what the Lord says:

"I have looked upon your nation with compassion and mercy. Though you are small in stature, you are mighty in heart. I have built you up and blessed your country so that soon Brussels will stand as a great leader among Christian nations. I have strategically placed Belgium and forced him to be multicultural and bilingual. You have consistently adapted and adjusted to the strong and dominate cultures surrounding your country. Yet you have remained loyal to Me by not corrupting your country with the abomination of Mecca. All of this has made you very talented and intuitive. You have received great

| 193

wisdom with your perseverance and have maintained a great foundation to build upon.

"Therefore, you will become a safety net for all Western Europe to flock to. I will use you in great and mighty ways. I will protect My Saints during the cleansing of your continent. Brussels, once the collapse of the European Union happens, your leadership will be well sought after. This will be a tumultuous period in Europe, and the dragon will use this time to hand his power over to the beast.

"Your stronghold for the Roman Catholic Church has slowly withered away just as it did during the Eighty Years' War. But your roots remain tangled in Jezebel's hair. Many of your countrymen fled during the war as they were forced to leave or join Catholicism. Instead of separating and dividing the Church, you should unite. Now is the time to regroup and fortify what faith you still have. It is okay to branch out and accept the Protestant Church. After all, they are your brothers. Do not flee or leave your homeland. I will fortify your lands and make you a stronghold for all Western Europe. I have blessed you for this purpose because of your allegiance to Me, regardless of the negative influences surrounding you. You are survivors! And you will be protected during the time of testing. Stand fast and keep hope, for I have a wonderful surprise coming to you!"

The Lord's Army Comes to Brussels with Fury

"I will raise up the Spaniard into your homeland, and he has tremendous power with him. He is surrounded by legions of Angels. For he has the descendants of Tarshish in his hand. He will reach down across the Southern Atlantic and gather his offspring. In an act of humility, he will hand his army over to Brussels, swearing allegiance by making a vow in the name of the Lord. The Spaniard will confirm much of your prayers, and because of his mighty American offspring and influence, he will save many souls for My sake during the time of testing. You will become like brothers, but it is you, Brussels, who will stand as the military leader.

I, Jesus Christ the Mighty, have spoken!"

Regrouping the Remnant in Brussels

This message came to Joshua from the Lord as instruction for the remnant in Belgium.

Listen to the Word of the Lord your King:

"These seven years will be seemingly endless. It will challenge everything that you are. It will rip at your soul, and your flesh will cry out in hatred to Me. But My Spirit will remain in you. I will keep you encouraged when outcomes look bleak. I will comfort you when fear has overwhelmed your mind. I will give you a sound mind with peace and dignity to die like soldiers in the Lord of Heaven's Armies. But I am making a promise to all of you here today: many will survive, and I will restore your land during the millennial reign. Your descendants will one day occupy the coast of Belgium as a providence of Israel. But until then, I command that all remnant head East and make your new home in Judah with the remnant of Jacob. There you will prosper and blend your culture and wisdom with that of Jacob's. You will adjust well and learn from each other because you are masters of adapting to new beginnings. This decree has been set, and I will embrace you at the gates of Jerusalem. For My love for you is great!

"As for the remnant of Tarshish that will come out of Brussels, this is My command:

"When I make My return, Tarshish and all of his descendants must set sail once again. For you are the great seafaring people, and many of you will be longing to go back home to the Americas. Just as Joseph brought his father, Jacob, to live with him in Egypt, so you descendants will bring your father, Tarshish, home with you to live in America. You will embrace each other as family who have been apart for centuries, and your love for each other will not allow you to separate. Therefore, set your sails West and meet King Timothy and his officials on the coast of the Carolinas. He will guide you back home to New Jerusalem. Trust your children Tarshish, it's okay. I have already appointed land for you and your descendants. Listen to Timothy. He is a good man and will have already embraced many of your brothers from Central America. Live among them and intermarry. He will show you the land I have promised your descendants and give it over to you during the end of his reign. Thank you for your service, Tarshish. You and your sons will always hold a special place in My kingdom for what you did. I love you all so much.

I, Jesus Christ the Mighty, have spoken."

**This is a gift from the Lord Jesus Christ.
To Him all the Glory**

Joshua David

References

Christ Jesus

The Holy Spirit

The Holy Bible

(King James Version, New Living Translation, American Standard Version, New International Version, New King James Version, Holman, English Standard Version, and International Standard Version.)

BibleGateway.com

Biblehub.com

Joshua David Ministries
PO Box 2242
Cookeville, TN 38501

Please visit our website:
www.joshuadavidministries.com

Email us:
joshuadavidministries@gmail.com

Follow on Facebook
@Joshua David Ministries

Follow on Twitter
@joshuadavidmin

CPSIA information can be obtained
at www.ICGtesting.com
Printed in the USA
JSHW010442090920
7721JS00004B/8

9 781977 209108